Campbell's

Simple 1-2-3™
Recipes

pil

Publications International, Ltd.

Pictured on the front cover: Swiss Vegetable Casserole *(page 91)*.
Pictured on the back cover *(clockwise from top right)*: Warm Spinach Dip *(page 23)*, Chicken Nacho Tacos *(page 77)* and Shrimp & Corn Chowder with Sun-Dried Tomatoes *(page 37)*.

Microwave Cooking: Microwave ovens vary in wattage. Use the cooking times as guidelines and check for doneness before adding more time.

Preparation/Cooking Times: Preparation times are based on the approximate amount of time required to assemble the recipe before cooking, baking, chilling or serving. These times include preparation steps such as measuring, chopping and mixing. The fact that some preparations and cooking can be done simultaneously is taken into account. Preparation of optional ingredients and serving suggestions is not included.

Contents

Appetizers & Snacks 4

Soup's On 24

30-Minute Dishes 40

Family Favorites 60

Holiday Fun 78

Vegetables & Sides 98

Sweet Treats 112

Beverages 126

Index 138

Appetizers & Snacks

Layered Pizza Dip

Prep: 10 minutes • **Bake:** 15 minutes • **Stand:** 5 minutes

- **1 cup part-skim ricotta cheese**
- **½ cup chopped pepperoni**
- **1 cup shredded mozzarella cheese (4 ounces)**
- **1 cup Prego® Traditional Italian Sauce, any variety**
- **Pepperidge Farm® Garlic Bread, any variety, heated according to package directions or Pepperidge Farm® Crackers, any variety**

1. Spread the ricotta cheese in an even layer in a 9-inch pie plate. Top with ¼ **cup** of the pepperoni and ½ **cup** mozzarella cheese. Carefully spread the Italian sauce over the cheese. Sprinkle with the remaining pepperoni and mozzarella cheese.

2. Bake at 375°F. for 15 minutes or until hot. Let stand for 5 minutes.

3. Serve with the garlic bread or crackers for dipping.

Makes about 3 cups

Kitchen Tip: Substitute or add any of the following toppings for the pepperoni: sliced pitted olives, sliced mushrooms, chopped sweet peppers **or** chopped onions.

Italiano Fondue

Prep: 5 minutes • **Cook:** 10 minutes • **Stand:** 5 minutes

1¾ **cups Prego® Traditional Italian Sauce**
¼ **cup dry red wine**
1 **cup shredded mozzarella cheese (4 ounces)**

Assorted Dippers: Warm Pepperidge Farm® Garlic Bread, cut into cubes, meatballs, sliced cooked Italian pork sausage, breaded mozzarella sticks **and/or** whole mushrooms

1. Stir the Italian sauce and wine in a 1-quart saucepan. Heat to a boil over medium heat, stirring often. Cook for 5 minutes for the alcohol to evaporate.

2. Pour the sauce into a fondue pot or slow cooker. Stir in the cheese. Let stand for 5 minutes for cheese to melt slightly.

3. Serve warm with *Assorted Dippers*.

Makes 2 cups

Appetizers & Snacks

Walnut-Cheddar Ball

Prep: 20 minutes • **Chill:** 2 hours

2 cups shredded Cheddar cheese
  (8 ounces)
½ cup finely chopped walnuts
¼ cup mayonnaise
1 medium green onion, chopped
  (about 2 tablespoons)
1 tablespoon Dijon-style mustard

1 teaspoon Worcestershire sauce
¼ cup chopped fresh parsley
1 tablespoon paprika
  Pepperidge Farm® Cracker
  Quartet **or** Cracker Trio
  Entertaining Collection Cracker
  Assortment

1. Mix the cheese, walnuts, mayonnaise, green onion, mustard and Worcestershire in a 1½-quart bowl.

2. Mix the parsley and paprika on a piece of wax paper. Shape the cheese mixture into a ball, then roll in the parsley mixture to coat. Wrap in plastic wrap. Refrigerate for 2 hours or until firm.

3. Unwrap the cheese ball and place on a serving plate. Serve with the crackers.

Makes 2 cups

Shrimp Dip

Prep: 5 minutes · **Chill:** 2 hours

1 **package (8 ounces) cream cheese, softened**
1 **can (10¾ ounces) Campbell's® Condensed Cream of Shrimp Soup**

½ **teaspoon Louisiana-style hot sauce**
¼ **cup finely chopped celery**
1 **tablespoon finely chopped onion**
Crackers, chips and/or fresh vegetables

Stir the cream cheese in a medium bowl until smooth. Stir in the soup, hot sauce, celery and onion. Refrigerate for 2 hours. Serve with the crackers for dipping.

Makes 18 servings

Porcupine Meatballs

Prep: 15 minutes • **Cook:** 20 minutes

1 **pound ground turkey**
2 **cups cooked brown or regular long-grain white rice**
1 **egg**
¾ **teaspoon dried oregano leaves, crushed**

½ **teaspoon garlic powder**
¼ **teaspoon ground black pepper**
1 **jar (1 pound 10 ounces) Prego® Traditional or Tomato, Basil & Garlic Italian Sauce**

1. Thoroughly mix the turkey, rice, egg, oregano, garlic powder and black pepper in a medium bowl.

2. Shape the mixture into **25** meatballs.

3. Heat the Italian sauce in a 12-inch skillet over medium-high heat. Add the meatballs in one layer. Heat to a boil. Reduce the heat to low. Cover and cook for 10 minutes or until meatballs are cooked through.

Makes 5 servings

Tex-Mex Toasts

Prep: 15 minutes • **Bake:** 10 minutes

1 package (9.5 ounces) Pepperidge
   Farm® Mozzarella Monterey
   Jack Texas Toast
6 tablespoons refried beans

Pace® Chunky Salsa
Sour cream
Chopped green onion

1. Prepare the Texas toast according to the package directions.

2. Spread **1 tablespoon** refried beans on **each** toast slice. Bake for 2 minutes or until the beans are hot.

3. Top the toast slices with the salsa, sour cream and green onion.

Makes 6 servings

Appetizers & Snacks

Spicy Grilled Quesadillas

Prep: 10 minutes • **Grill:** 5 minutes • **Stand:** 2 minutes

8 flour tortillas (8-inch)
2 cups shredded Cheddar cheese
   (about 8 ounces)
1 jar (16 ounces) Pace® Picante
   Sauce

1 cup diced cooked chicken
4 medium green onions, chopped
   (about ½ cup)
   Vegetable oil
1 container (8 ounces) sour cream

1. Top **each** of **4** tortillas with ½ **cup** cheese, ¼ **cup** picante sauce, ¼ **cup** chicken and **2 tablespoons** green onions. Brush the edges of the tortillas with water. Top with the remaining tortillas and press the edges to seal.

2. Lightly oil the grill rack and heat the grill to medium. Brush the tops of the quesadillas with oil. Place the quesadillas, oil-side down, on the grill rack. Brush the other side of the quesadillas with oil. Grill the quesadillas for 5 minutes or until the cheese is melted, turning the quesadillas over once during grilling. Remove the quesadillas from the grill and let stand 2 minutes.

3. Cut the quesadillas into wedges. Serve with the remaining picante sauce and sour cream.

Makes 4 servings

Kitchen Tip: Quesadillas are an easy way to turn leftover meat and shredded cheese into a whole new meal. You can even combine different varieties of shredded cheese to make the 2 cups needed in this recipe.

Hot Artichoke Dip

Prep: 10 minutes • **Bake:** 30 minutes

1 **cup mayonnaise**
1 **cup sour cream**
1 **can (14 ounces) artichoke hearts,**
   drained and chopped
¼ **cup chopped roasted sweet**
   peppers

¼ **cup grated Parmesan cheese**
1 **can (2.8 ounces) French fried**
   onions (1⅓ cups)
   Assorted Pepperidge Farm®
   Crackers

1. Heat the oven to 375°F. Mix the mayonnaise, sour cream, artichokes, peppers, cheese and ⅔ **cup** onions in 9-inch pie plate or 1-quart baking dish. Bake for 25 minutes or until hot.

2. Top with the remaining onions. Bake for 5 minutes more or until golden.

3. Serve with the crackers for dipping.

Makes 3 cups

Grilled Bruschetta

Prep: 5 minutes • **Stand:** 15 minutes • **Grill:** 2 minutes

3 tablespoons olive oil
2 tablespoons red wine vinegar
2 cloves garlic, minced
½ teaspoon cracked black pepper
2 tablespoons chopped fresh
  parsley **or** basil leaves

2 medium tomatoes, chopped
  (about 2 cups)
1 package (11.25 ounces)
  Pepperidge Farm® Parmesan
  Texas Toast **or** Garlic Texas
  Toast

1. Stir the oil, vinegar, garlic, black pepper, parsley and tomatoes in a medium bowl. Let stand for 15 minutes.

2. Lightly oil the grill rack and heat the grill to medium. Grill the toast slices for 2 minutes or until they're browned on both sides and heated through.

3. Divide the tomato mixture among the toast slices. Serve immediately.

Makes 8 servings

Kitchen Tip: Omit the garlic if using Garlic Texas Toast.

Cheesy Vegetable Triangles

Prep: 15 minutes

¼ **cup light whipped cream cheese**
4 **slices Pepperidge Farm® Very Thin Wheat or White Bread, toasted**

1 **cup thinly sliced cucumber**
¼ **cup diced canned beets**
Fresh dill sprigs

1. Spread **about 1 tablespoon** of the cream cheese on **each** toast slice.

2. Divide the cucumber and beets among the toast slices.

3. Cut the sandwiches diagonally into quarters. Top **each** quarter with a dill sprig. Serve immediately.

Makes 16 appetizers

Salmon Bites

Prep: 15 minutes

¼ cup lowfat mayonnaise
2 teaspoons fresh lemon juice
1 can (about 6 ounces) white **or** pink salmon, drained and flaked

1 medium tomato, cut in half and thinly sliced
4 slices Pepperidge Farm® Very Thin Wheat **or** White Bread, toasted
¼ cup very thinly sliced red onion

1. Stir the mayonnaise and lemon juice in a medium bowl. Stir in the salmon.

2. Divide the tomato slices and salmon mixture among the toast slices and top with the red onion.

3. Cut the sandwiches diagonally into quarters. Serve immediately.

Makes 16 appetizers

Seafood & Cilantro Sandwiches

Prep: 20 minutes

¼ cup light cream cheese, softened
1 teaspoon chopped fresh cilantro
1 teaspoon fresh lime juice
4 slices Pepperidge Farm® Very Thin
   Wheat **or** White Bread, toasted

½ cup imitation crabmeat (surimi),
   broken into bite-size pieces
Fresh cilantro sprigs

1. Mix the cream cheese, cilantro and lime juice in a small bowl.

2. Spread **about 1 tablespoon** of the cheese mixture on **each** toast slice. Divide the crabmeat among the toast slices.

3. Cut the sandwiches diagonally into quarters. Top **each** quarter with a cilantro sprig. Serve immediately.

Makes 16 appetizers

Sausage-Stuffed Mushrooms

Prep: 25 minutes • **Bake:** 10 minutes

24 **medium mushrooms**	½ **cup dry bread crumbs**
2 **tablespoons butter, melted**	**Chopped fresh cilantro leaves or**
¼ **pound bulk pork sausage**	**fresh parsley**
1 **cup Pace® Picante Sauce**	

1. Heat the oven to 425°F. Remove the stems from the mushrooms. Chop enough stems to make **1 cup**. Brush the mushroom caps with the butter and place top-side down in a shallow baking pan.

2. Cook the sausage and the chopped mushroom stems in a 10-inch skillet over medium-high heat until the sausage is well browned, stirring often to separate the meat. Pour off any fat.

3. Add ½ **cup** picante sauce and the bread crumbs to the skillet and mix lightly. Spoon **about 1 tablespoon** sausage mixture into **each** mushroom cap.

4. Bake for 10 minutes or until the mushrooms are hot. Top **each** with **1 teaspoon** picante sauce and sprinkle with the cilantro.

Makes 24 appetizers

Kitchen Tip: Cut a thin slice from the top of **each** mushroom cap to keep the caps from rolling in the pan.

Kitchen Tip: To make ahead, prepare as directed above through Step 3. Cover and refrigerate the stuffed mushrooms up to 24 hours. Bake as directed in Step 4.

Single-Serve Southwest Dip Cups

Prep: 20 minutes

24 foil baking cups (2½ inch)
1 can (about 16 ounces) refried
   beans
2 jars (11 ounces **each**) Pace®
   Chunky Salsa
3 medium avocados, peeled, pitted
   and chopped (about 1½ cups)

1½ cups shredded Cheddar cheese
   (about 6 ounces)
1½ cups sour cream
½ cup chopped fresh cilantro leaves
   Bite-sized tortilla chips

1. Place the foil cups onto a serving platter.

2. Layer **about 1 tablespoon each** beans, salsa, avocado and cheese into **each** cup. Top **each** with **about 1 tablespoon** sour cream and **about 1 teaspoon** cilantro. Serve with the tortilla chips for dipping.

Makes 24 servings

Kitchen Tip: Stop traffic jams around the dip bowl! Spoon a few tablespoons of favorite dips into foil baking cups. Guests can cruise by the serving table and pick up a dip cup and some dippers and move on to mingle with other guests.

Caponata Appetizer

Prep: 15 minutes • **Cook:** 55 minutes

1 tablespoon vegetable oil
1 large eggplant, cut into cubes
  (about 8 cups)
1 Spanish onion, chopped
  (about 2 cups)
1 large red pepper, chopped
  (about 1 cup)
2 cloves garlic, minced

1 can (10¾ ounces) Campbell's®
  Condensed Tomato Soup
  (Regular **or** Healthy Request®)
1⅓ cups water
1 teaspoon dried oregano leaves,
  crushed
  Assorted Pepperidge Farm®
  crackers

1. Heat the oil in a 6-quart saucepot over medium-high heat. Add the eggplant, onion, red pepper and garlic and cook for 10 minutes or until the eggplant is tender-crisp.

2. Stir in the soup and water and heat to a boil. Reduce the heat to low. Cover and cook for 40 minutes or until the vegetables are tender.

3. Stir in the oregano. Serve the caponata warm or at room temperature with the crackers.

Makes 20 servings

Kitchen Tip: Leftover caponata is delicious tossed with hot cooked pasta topped off with some grated Parmesan cheese.

Fiesta Tortilla Roll-Ups

Prep: 15 minutes • **Chill:** 30 minutes

1 **package (8 ounces) light cream cheese, softened**

1 **jar (16 ounces) Pace® Picante Sauce**

1 **green onion, chopped (about 2 tablespoons)**

6 **flour tortillas (8-inch), warmed**

1 **cup shredded spinach leaves or romaine lettuce**

6 **thin slices cooked turkey breast, cut in half**

¼ **cup chopped pimientos or red peppers**

1. Stir the cream cheese, picante sauce and onion in a medium bowl.

2. Spread **about ¼ cup** cheese mixture onto **each** tortilla to within ½ inch of the edge. Divide the spinach among the tortillas. Top **each** with ½ **slice** turkey and **2 teaspoons** pimientos. Roll up the tortillas around the filling. Place the rolls seam-side down in a 3-quart shallow baking dish. Cover and refrigerate for 30 minutes.

3. Cut **each** roll into **6** slices. Secure **each** slice with a toothpick. Serve with additional picante sauce for dipping.

Makes 36 appetizers

Kitchen Tip: To soften the cream cheese, remove the wrapper and place the cheese on a microwaveable plate. Microwave on HIGH for 15 seconds.

Game-Winning Drumsticks

Prep: 10 minutes • **Chill:** 4 hours • **Cook:** 1 hour

**15 chicken drumsticks (about
4 pounds)**
1¾ cups Swanson® Chicken Stock

½ cup Dijon-style mustard
**⅓ cup Italian-seasoned dry bread
crumbs**

1. Place the chicken in a single layer into a 15×10-inch disposable foil pan.

2. Stir the stock and mustard in a small bowl. Pour the stock mixture over the chicken and turn to coat. Sprinkle the bread crumbs over the chicken. Cover the pan and refrigerate for 4 hours.

3. Bake at 375°F. for 1 hour or until the chicken is cooked through. Serve hot or at room temperature.

Makes 6 servings

Kitchen Tip: Keep disposable foil pans on hand for convenience to tote casseroles to friends' parties or covered-dish suppers. As a safety reminder, be sure to support the bottom of the filled pan when handling them in and out of the oven.

Warm French Onion Dip with Crusty Bread

Prep: 15 minutes • **Bake:** 30 minutes

1 can (10½ ounces) Campbell's®
   Condensed French Onion Soup
1 package (8 ounces) cream cheese,
   softened

1 cup shredded mozzarella cheese
Crusty bread cubes **or** crackers

1. Heat the oven to 375°F. Stir the soup and cream cheese in a medium bowl until it's smooth. Stir in the mozzarella cheese. Spread in a 1½-quart shallow baking dish.

2. Bake for 30 minutes or until the mixture is hot and bubbling.

3. Serve with the bread for dipping.

Makes 2 cups

Kitchen Tip: To soften the cream cheese, remove from the wrapper and place on a microwavable plate. Microwave on HIGH for 15 seconds.

Warm Spinach Dip

Prep: 15 minutes • **Cook:** 15 minutes

Vegetable cooking spray
1 medium onion, chopped
    (about ½ cup)
2 packages (10 ounces **each**) frozen
    chopped spinach, thawed and
    well drained

2 tablespoons all-purpose flour
1 cup milk
1 cup Pace® Picante Sauce
4 ounces shredded part-skim
    mozzarella cheese (about 1 cup)
Tortilla chips **or** fresh vegetables

1. Spray a 2-quart saucepan with the cooking spray and heat over medium heat for 1 minute. Add the onion and cook until it's tender, stirring occasionally.

2. Stir the spinach and flour in the skillet. Gradually stir the milk in the skillet. Cook and stir until the mixture boils and thickens. Stir in the picante sauce and cheese and cook until the cheese is melted. Serve with the tortilla chips for dipping.

Makes 32 servings

Soup's On

Southwestern Chicken & White Bean Soup

Prep: 15 minutes • **Cook:** 8 hours

- 1 **tablespoon vegetable oil**
- 1 **pound skinless, boneless chicken breast, cut into 1-inch pieces**
- 1¾ **cups Swanson® Chicken Broth (Regular, Natural Goodness® or Certified Organic)**
- 1 **cup Pace® Picante Sauce**
- 3 **cloves garlic, minced**
- 2 **teaspoons ground cumin**
- 1 **can (about 16 ounces) small white beans, rinsed and drained**
- 1 **cup frozen whole kernel corn**
- 1 **large onion, chopped (about 1 cup)**

1. Heat the oil in a 10-inch skillet over medium-high heat. Add the chicken and cook until it's well browned, stirring often.

2. Stir the chicken, broth, picante sauce, garlic, cumin, beans, corn and onion in a 3½-quart slow cooker.

3. Cover and cook on LOW for 8 to 9 hours* or until the chicken is cooked through.

Makes 6 servings

Or on HIGH for 4 to 5 hours.

Spicy Peanut Soup

Prep: 15 minutes • **Cook:** 30 minutes

2 tablespoons vegetable oil
1 large onion, diced (about 2 cups)
2 large carrots, diced (about 1 cup)
1 tablespoon minced fresh ginger
¼ teaspoon ground red pepper
6 cups Swanson® Chicken Broth
   (Regular, Natural Goodness® or
   Certified Organic)

2 large sweet potatoes, peeled and
   diced (about 3 cups)
1 cup creamy peanut butter
⅓ cup sliced green onions **or** chives
⅓ cup chopped peanuts

1. Heat the oil in a 4-quart saucepan over medium heat. Add onion, carrots and ginger and cook until they're tender-crisp. Add the red pepper and cook for 1 minute.

2. Stir the broth and sweet potatoes into the saucepan. Heat to a boil. Cover and reduce the heat to low. Cook for 20 minutes or until vegetables are tender. Stir in the peanut butter.

3. Place ⅓ of the broth mixture in an electric blender or food processor container. Cover and blend until smooth. Pour into a large bowl. Repeat the blending process twice more with the remaining broth mixture. Return all of the puréed mixture to the saucepan. Cook over medium heat until the mixture is hot. Season to taste. Divide the soup among **8** serving bowls. Top **each** serving of soup with the green onions and peanuts.

Makes 8 servings

Sausage and Spinach Soup

Prep: 5 minutes • **Cook:** 20 minutes

Vegetable cooking spray
½ pound sweet Italian pork sausage, cut into ¾-inch pieces
4 cups Swanson® Chicken Broth (Regular, Natural Goodness® or Certified Organic)
½ teaspoon dried oregano leaves, crushed

1 medium onion, chopped (about ½ cup)
1 medium carrot, sliced (about ½ cup)
2 cups coarsely chopped fresh spinach leaves

1. Spray a 4-quart saucepan with cooking spray and heat over medium-high heat for 1 minute. Add the sausage and cook until it's well browned, stirring often. Pour off any fat.

2. Stir in the broth, oregano, onion and carrot. Heat to a boil. Reduce the heat to low. Cover and cook for 10 minutes or until the vegetables are tender.

3. Stir in the spinach and cook for 1 minute.

Makes 5 servings

Creamy Beet Soup

Prep: 10 minutes • **Cook:** 20 minutes

2 tablespoons butter

3 small onions, chopped (about 1½ cups)

1 potato, peeled and chopped (about 1 cup)

1 clove garlic, minced

2 cans (14.5 ounces **each**) sliced beets, undrained

3 cups Swanson® Chicken Broth (Regular, Natural Goodness® **or** Certified Organic)

1 tablespoon chopped fresh dill weed **or** 1 teaspoon dried dill weed, crushed

¼ teaspoon ground black pepper Sour cream

1. Heat the butter in a 4-quart saucepan over medium heat. Add the onions and cook until they're tender-crisp. Add the potato and garlic and cook for 1 minute.

2. Drain the liquid from the beets and reserve **1 cup** beet juice. Add the beets and broth to the saucepan and heat to a boil. Reduce the heat to low. Cover and cook for 15 minutes more or until the potato is tender.

3. Place ½ of the broth mixture into an electric blender or food processor container. Cover and blend until smooth. Pour into a medium bowl. Repeat the blending process with the remaining broth mixture. Return all of the puréed mixture to the saucepan. Stir in the reserved beet juice, dill and black pepper. Cook over medium heat until the mixture is hot. Serve with sour cream.

Makes 8 servings

Kitchen Tip: To serve cold, cover and refrigerate 2 hours or until cold.

Roasted Tomato & Barley Soup

Prep: 10 minutes • **Roast:** 25 minutes • **Cook:** 40 minutes

1 can (about 28 ounces) diced tomatoes, undrained
2 large onions, diced (about 2 cups)
2 cloves garlic, minced
2 tablespoons olive oil

4 cups Swanson® Chicken Broth (Regular, Natural Goodness® or Certified Organic)
2 stalks celery, diced (about 1 cup)
½ cup **uncooked** pearl barley
2 tablespoons chopped fresh parsley

1. Heat the oven to 425°F. Drain the tomatoes, reserving the juice. Place the tomatoes, onions and garlic into a 17×11-inch roasting pan. Pour the oil over the vegetables and toss to coat. Bake for 25 minutes.

2. Place the roasted vegetables into a 3-quart saucepan. Stir in the reserved tomato juice, broth, celery and barley and heat to a boil. Reduce the heat to low. Cover and cook for 35 minutes or until the barley is tender. Stir in the parsley.

Makes 8 servings

Simply Special Seafood Chowder

Prep: 10 minutes • **Cook:** 20 minutes

1 tablespoon olive oil **or** vegetable oil

1 medium bulb fennel, trimmed, halved and thinly sliced (about 2 cups)

1 medium onion, chopped (about ½ cup)

1 teaspoon dried thyme leaves, crushed

5 cups water

1¾ cups Swanson® Vegetable Broth (Regular **or** Certified Organic)

1 can (10¾ ounces) Campbell's® Condensed Tomato Soup

1 package (about 10 ounces) frozen whole baby carrots, thawed (about 1½ cups)

½ pound fresh **or** thawed frozen firm white fish fillet (cod, haddock **or** halibut), cut into 2-inch pieces

½ pound fresh large shrimp, peeled and deveined

¾ pound mussels (about 12), well scrubbed and beards removed

Freshly ground black pepper

1. Heat the oil in a 6-quart saucepot over medium heat. Add the fennel, onion and thyme and cook until they're tender. Stir the water, broth, soup and carrots in the saucepot and heat to a boil.

2. Add the fish. Cover and cook over medium heat for 2 minutes. Discard any open or cracked mussels. Add the shrimp and mussels. Cover and simmer for 3 minutes or until the fish flakes easily with a fork, the shrimp are pink and the mussels open. Discard any mussels that do not open. Sprinkle with black pepper.

Makes 6 servings

Creamy Citrus Tomato Soup with Pesto Croutons

Prep: 10 minutes • **Cook:** 5 minutes

1 can (10¾ ounces) Campbell's® Condensed Tomato Soup (Regular or Healthy Request®)	**1 tablespoon lemon juice**
1 cup milk	**6 tablespoons prepared pesto sauce**
½ cup light cream or half-and-half	**6 slices French or Italian bread, ½-inch thick, toasted**

1. Stir the soup, milk, cream and lemon juice in a 2-quart saucepan. Heat over medium heat until the mixture is hot and bubbling.

2. Spread **1 tablespoon** pesto on **each** toast slice.

3. Divide the soup among **6** serving bowls. Float **1** pesto crouton in **each** bowl of soup.

Makes 6 servings

Kitchen Tip: If you have some goat cheese on hand, spread a little on the toast slice before topping with the pesto.

Slow-Simmered Chicken Rice Soup

Prep: 10 minutes • **Cook:** 7 hours 15 minutes

½ cup **uncooked** wild rice
½ cup **uncooked** regular long-grain
  white rice
1 tablespoon vegetable oil
5¼ cups Swanson® Chicken Broth
  (Regular, Natural Goodness® **or**
  Certified Organic)
2 teaspoons dried thyme leaves,
  crushed

¼ teaspoon crushed red pepper
2 stalks celery, coarsely chopped
  (about 1 cup)
1 medium onion, chopped
  (about ½ cup)
1 pound skinless, boneless chicken
  breasts, cut into cubes
Sour cream (optional)
Chopped green onions (optional)

1. Stir the wild rice, white rice and oil in a 3½-quart slow cooker. Cover and cook on HIGH for 15 minutes.

2. Add the broth, thyme, red pepper, celery, onion and chicken to the cooker. Turn the heat to LOW. Cover and cook for 7 to 8 hours* or until the chicken is cooked through.

3. Serve with the sour cream and green onions, if desired.

Makes 8 servings

*Or on HIGH for 4 to 5 hours.

Kitchen Tip: Speed preparation by substituting 3 cans (4.5 ounces **each**) Swanson® Premium Chunk Chicken Breast, drained, for the raw chicken.

White Bean with Fennel Soup

Prep: 15 minutes • **Cook:** 7 hours

4 cups Swanson® Vegetable Broth
   (Regular **or** Certified Organic)
⅛ teaspoon ground black pepper
1 small bulb fennel, trimmed and
   sliced (about 2 cups)
1 small onion, chopped
   (about ½ cup)

2 cloves garlic, minced
1 package (10 ounces) frozen leaf
   spinach, thawed
1 can (about 14.5 ounces) diced
   tomatoes, undrained
1 can (about 16 ounces) white
   kidney beans (cannellini),
   undrained

1. Stir the broth, black pepper, fennel, onion and garlic in a 5½- to 6-quart
slow cooker.

2. Cover and cook on LOW for 6 to 7 hours.

3. Add the spinach, tomatoes and beans. Turn the heat to HIGH. Cover and
cook for 1 hour more or until the vegetables are tender.

Makes 6 servings

Slow Cooker Tuscan Beef Stew

Prep: 15 minutes • **Cook:** 8 hours 10 minutes

1 can (10¾ ounces) Campbell's® Condensed Tomato Soup

1 can (10½ ounces) Campbell's® Condensed Beef Broth

½ cup Burgundy wine **or** other dry red wine **or** water

1 teaspoon dried Italian seasoning, crushed

½ teaspoon garlic powder

1 can (14.5 ounces) diced tomatoes with Italian herbs

3 large carrots, cut into 1-inch pieces (about 2 cups)

2 pounds beef for stew, cut into 1-inch pieces

2 cans (about 15 ounces **each**) white kidney beans (cannellini), rinsed and drained

1. Stir the soup, broth, wine, Italian seasoning, garlic powder, tomatoes, carrots and beef in a 3½-quart slow cooker.

2. Cover and cook on LOW for 8 to 9 hours* or until the beef is fork-tender.

3. Stir in the beans. Increase the heat to HIGH. Cook for 10 minutes or until the mixture is hot.

Makes 8 servings

Or on HIGH for 4 to 5 hours.

Creamy Irish Potato Soup

Prep: 15 minutes • **Cook:** 30 minutes

2 tablespoons butter	½ cup water
4 medium green onions, sliced (about ½ cup)	⅛ teaspoon ground black pepper
1 stalk celery, sliced (about ½ cup)	3 medium potatoes, sliced ¼-inch thick (about 3 cups)
1¾ cups Swanson® Chicken Broth (Regular, Natural Goodness® or Certified Organic)	1½ cups milk
	Sliced chives **or** green onions (optional)

1. Heat the butter in a 2-quart saucepan over medium-high heat. Add the green onions and celery and cook until tender.

2. Stir the broth, water, black pepper and potatoes into the saucepan. Heat to a boil. Reduce the heat to low. Cover and cook for 15 minutes more or until the potatoes are tender. Remove from heat.

3. Place ½ of the broth mixture and ¾ **cup** of the milk into an electric blender container. Cover and blend until smooth. Pour into a medium bowl. Repeat the blending process with the remaining broth mixture and remaining milk. Return all of the puréed mixture to the saucepan. Cook over medium heat until the mixture is hot. Sprinkle with chives, if desired.

Makes 5 servings

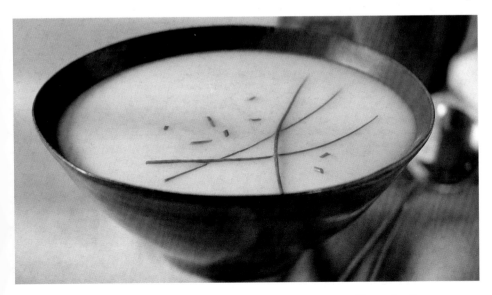

Chipotle Chili

Prep: 15 minutes • **Cook:** 8 hours

1 jar (16 ounces) Pace® Picante Sauce
1 cup water
2 tablespoons chili powder
1 teaspoon ground chipotle chile
   pepper
1 large onion, chopped (about 1 cup)

2 pounds beef for stew, cut into
   ½-inch pieces
1 can (about 19 ounces) red kidney
   beans, rinsed and drained
   Shredded Cheddar cheese
   (optional)
   Sour cream (optional)

1. Stir the picante sauce, water, chili powder, chipotle pepper, onion, beef and beans in a 3½-quart slow cooker.

2. Cover and cook on LOW for 8 to 9 hours* or until the beef is fork-tender. Serve with the cheese and sour cream, if desired.

Makes 8 servings

*Or on HIGH for 4 to 5 hours.

Shrimp & Corn Chowder with Sun-Dried Tomatoes

Prep: 10 minutes · **Cook:** 20 minutes

1　can (10¾ ounces) Campbell's®
　　Condensed Cream of Potato
　　Soup
1½　cups half-and-half
2　cups whole kernel corn, drained
2　tablespoons sun-dried tomatoes
　　cut into strips

1　cup small **or** medium peeled and
　　deveined cooked shrimp
2　tablespoons chopped fresh
　　chives
　　Ground black pepper

1. Heat the soup, half-and-half, corn and tomatoes in a 3-quart saucepan over medium heat to a boil. Reduce the heat to low. Cook for 10 minutes.

2. Stir in the shrimp and chives and cook until the mixture is hot and bubbling. Season with the black pepper.

Makes 4 servings

Kitchen Tip: For a lighter version, use skim milk instead of the half-and-half.

Soup's On ·37·

Hearty Bean & Barley Soup

Prep: 15 minutes • **Cook:** 40 minutes

1 tablespoon olive oil
2 large carrots, coarsely chopped
   (about 1 cup)
2 stalks celery, sliced (about 1 cup)
1 large onion, chopped (about 1 cup)
3½ cups Swanson® Vegetable Broth
   (Regular **or** Certified Organic)

1 can (about 15 ounces) red kidney
   beans, rinsed and drained
1 can (about 14.5 ounces) diced
   tomatoes
¼ cup **uncooked** pearl barley
2 cups firmly packed chopped fresh
   spinach leaves
   Ground black pepper

1. Heat the oil in a 4-quart saucepan over medium-high heat. Add the carrots, celery and onion. Cook and stir until the vegetables are tender.

2. Stir the broth, beans, tomatoes and barley in the saucepan. Heat to a boil. Reduce the heat to low. Cover and cook for 30 minutes or until the barley is tender.

3. Stir in the spinach and season to taste with black pepper. Cook until the spinach is tender.

Makes 6 servings

Spaghetti Soup

Prep: 15 minutes • **Cook:** 30 minutes

2 tablespoons vegetable oil
½ pound skinless, boneless chicken breast halves, cut into cubes
1 medium onion, chopped (about ½ cup)
1 large carrot, chopped (about ½ cup)
1 stalk celery, finely chopped (about ½ cup)
2 cloves garlic, minced

4 cups Swanson® Chicken Broth (Regular, Natural Goodness® **or** Certified Organic)
1 can (10¾ ounces) Campbell's® Condensed Tomato Soup (Regular **or** Healthy Request®)
1 cup water
3 ounces **uncooked** spaghetti, broken into 1-inch pieces
2 tablespoons chopped fresh parsley (optional)

1. Heat **1 tablespoon** of the oil in a 6-quart saucepot over medium-high heat. Add the chicken and cook until it's well browned, stirring often. Remove the chicken from the saucepot.

2. Add the remaining oil to the saucepot and heat over medium heat. Add the onion and cook for 1 minute. Add the carrot and cook for 1 minute. Add the celery and garlic and cook for 1 minute.

3. Stir in the broth, soup and water. Heat to a boil. Stir in the spaghetti. Cook for 10 minutes or until the spaghetti is tender. Stir in the chicken and parsley, if desired, and cook until the mixture is hot and bubbling.

Makes 4 servings

30-Minute Dishes

Southwest Chicken with Fresh Greens

Prep: 10 minutes · **Cook:** 10 minutes

- **1 tablespoon chili powder**
- **1 teaspoon ground cumin**
- **6 skinless, boneless chicken breasts (about 1½ pounds), cut into strips**
- **1 tablespoon olive oil**
- **1 cup Pace® Picante Sauce**
- **¼ cup water**
- **1 bag (about 7 ounces) mixed salad greens**

1. Stir the chili powder and cumin in a medium bowl. Add the chicken and toss to coat.

2. Heat the oil in a heavy 12-inch skillet over high heat. Add the chicken and cook until it's blackened and cooked through, stirring often. Remove the chicken from the skillet.

3. Stir the picante sauce and water in the skillet and cook until the mixture is hot and bubbling. Divide the greens among **6** plates. Top with the chicken and sauce mixture.

Makes 6 servings

Italian Fish Fillets

Prep: 10 minutes • **Bake:** 10 minutes

2 slices Pepperidge Farm® White
   Sandwich Bread, torn into
   pieces
⅓ cup grated Parmesan cheese
1 clove garlic
½ teaspoon dried thyme leaves,
   crushed

⅛ teaspoon ground black pepper
2 tablespoons olive oil
8 fish fillets (3 to 4 ounces **each**)
   tilapia **or** other firm white fish
   fillets (cod, haddock **or** halibut)
   (about 2 pounds)
1 egg, beaten

1. Place bread, cheese, garlic, thyme and black pepper in blender or food
processor. Cover and blend until fine crumbs form. Slowly add olive oil and
blend until moistened.

2. Arrange fish fillets in large shallow roasting pan. Brush with egg. Divide
bread crumb mixture evenly over fillets.

3. Bake at 400°F. for 10 minutes or until fish flakes easily when tested with a
fork and crumb topping is golden.

Makes 8 servings

Chicken & Black Bean Quesadillas

Prep: 15 minutes • **Cook:** 5 minutes • **Bake:** 5 minutes

1 can (10¾ ounces) Campbell's®
   Condensed Cheddar Cheese
   Soup
½ cup Pace® Picante Sauce
1 cup rinsed and drained canned
   black beans

2 cans (4.5 ounces **each**) Swanson®
   Premium White Chunk Chicken
   Breast in Water, drained
10 flour tortillas (8-inch), warmed
   Fiesta Rice

1. Heat the oven to 425°F.

2. Heat the soup, picante sauce, beans and chicken in a 1-quart saucepan over medium heat until the mixture is hot and bubbling.

3. Place the tortillas onto 2 baking sheets. Spread **about ⅓ cup** soup mixture onto **half** of **each** tortilla to within ½ inch of the edge. Brush the edges of the tortillas with water. Fold the tortillas over the filling and press the edges to seal.

4. Bake for 5 minutes or until the filling is hot. Cut the quesadillas in half, making **20** pieces. Serve with the *Fiesta Rice*.

Makes 4 servings

Fiesta Rice: Heat **1 can** (10½ ounces) Campbell's® Condensed Chicken Broth, ½ **cup** water and ½ **cup** Pace® Picante Sauce in a 2-quart saucepan over medium-high heat to a boil. Stir in **2 cups uncooked** instant white rice. Cover the saucepan and remove from the heat. Let stand for 5 minutes.

Grilled Fish Steaks
with Chunky Tomato Sauce

Prep: 15 minutes • **Grill:** 10 minutes

Vegetable cooking spray
1 stalk celery, chopped (about ½ cup)
1 small green pepper, chopped
   (about ½ cup)
1 medium onion, chopped
   (about ½ cup)
½ teaspoon dried thyme leaves,
   crushed
¼ teaspoon garlic powder **or** 2 cloves
   garlic, minced

1 can (10¾ ounces) Campbell's®
   Healthy Request® Condensed
   Tomato Soup
2 tablespoons lemon juice
⅛ teaspoon hot pepper sauce
   (optional)
6 swordfish **or** tuna steaks, 1-inch
   thick (about 2¼ pounds)

1. Spray a 2-quart saucepan with cooking spray. Heat over medium heat for 1 minute. Add the celery, green pepper, onion, thyme and garlic powder and cook until tender, stirring often.

2. Stir in the soup, lemon juice and hot pepper sauce. Heat through, stirring occasionally.

3. Lightly oil the grill rack and heat the grill to medium. Grill the fish, uncovered, for 10 minutes or until the fish flakes easily when tested with a fork, turning once during cooking. Serve the sauce over the fish.

Makes 6 servings

Beef & Bean Burritos

Prep: 5 minutes • **Cook:** 15 minutes

1 **pound ground beef**
1 **can (10¾ ounces) Campbell's®**
   Condensed Bean with Bacon
   Soup

1 **cup Pace® Picante Sauce**
8 **flour tortillas (8-inch), warmed**
   Shredded Cheddar cheese
   Sour cream (optional)

1. Cook the beef in a 10-inch skillet over medium-high heat until it's well browned, stirring often to separate the meat. Pour off any fat.

2. Stir the soup and picante sauce in the skillet and cook until the mixture is hot and bubbling, mashing the beans with a fork.

3. Spoon **about ½ cup** beef mixture down the center of **each** tortilla. Top with the cheese, additional picante sauce and sour cream, if desired. Fold the tortillas around the filling.

Makes 8 burritos

Grilled Pork in Pita

Prep: 5 minutes • **Grill:** 15 minutes

¾ cup Pace® Picante Sauce
½ cup plain yogurt
1 teaspoon lime juice
¼ teaspoon garlic powder **or**
   2 cloves garlic, minced

1 pound boneless pork chops,
   ¾-inch thick
6 pita breads (6-inch), warmed
1 cup shredded lettuce
1 medium green onion, sliced
   (about 2 tablespoons)

1. Stir **3 tablespoons** picante sauce, yogurt and lime juice in a small bowl. Cover and refrigerate until ready to serve. Stir the remaining picante sauce and garlic powder in a small bowl.

2. Lightly oil the grill rack and heat the grill to medium-high. Grill the pork for 15 minutes or until it's cooked through, turning and brushing often with the picante sauce mixture. Discard any remaining picante sauce mixture.

3. Slice the pork into thin strips. Divide the pork among the pita breads. Top with the yogurt mixture, lettuce and green onion. Fold the pitas around the filling.

Makes 6 servings

Kitchen Tip: To warm the pita breads, wrap them in a plain paper towel. Microwave on HIGH for 1 minute or until they're warm.

Tomato-Basil Chicken

Prep: 5 minutes • **Cook:** 20 minutes

1 tablespoon vegetable oil	**2** tablespoons grated Parmesan
1½ pounds skinless, boneless chicken	cheese
breast halves (about 4 to 6)	**½** teaspoon dried basil leaves,
1 can (10¾ ounces) Campbell's®	crushed
Condensed Tomato Soup	**¼** teaspoon garlic powder **or**
(Regular **or** Healthy Request®)	2 cloves garlic, minced
½ cup milk	**3** cups medium tube-shaped pasta
	(ziti), cooked and drained

1. Heat the oil in a 10-inch skillet over medium-high heat. Add the chicken and cook for 10 minutes or until it's well browned on both sides. Remove the chicken and set aside.

2. Stir in the soup, milk, cheese, basil and garlic powder. Heat to a boil. Return the chicken to the skillet and reduce the heat to low. Cover and cook for 5 minutes or until the chicken is cooked through.

3. Serve with the pasta.

Makes 6 servings

French Onion Burgers

Prep: 5 minutes • **Cook:** 20 minutes

1 pound ground beef
1 can (10½ ounces) Campbell's®
    Condensed French Onion Soup
4 slices cheese

4 Pepperidge Farm® Classic
    Sandwich Buns with Sesame
    Seeds, split

1. Shape the beef into **4** (½-inch-thick) burgers.

2. Heat a 10-inch skillet over medium-high heat. Add the burgers and cook until well browned on both sides. Remove the burgers from the skillet. Pour off any fat.

3. Stir the soup in the skillet and heat to a boil. Return the burgers to the skillet. Reduce the heat to low. Cover and cook for 5 minutes or until desired doneness. Top the burgers with the cheese and cook until the cheese is melted. Serve the burgers on the buns with the soup mixture for dipping.

Makes 4 servings

Kitchen Tip: You can also serve these burgers in a bowl atop a mound of hot mashed potatoes with some of the soup mixture poured over.

Layered Chicken Parmesan

Prep: 5 minutes • **Bake:** 10 minutes

2 cups Prego® Traditional Italian
   Sauce
4 fully cooked breaded chicken
   cutlets

4 thin slices cooked ham
1 cup shredded mozzarella cheese
2 tablespoons grated Parmesan
   cheese

1. Spread **1 cup** of the Italian sauce in an 11×8-inch (2-quart) shallow baking dish.

2. Place the chicken cutlets over the sauce. Spoon ¼ **cup** of the remaining sauce down the center of **each** cutlet. Top **each** with **1** slice ham and ¼ **cup** of the mozzarella cheese. Sprinkle with the Parmesan cheese.

3. Bake at 425°F. for 10 minutes or until the cheese melts and the sauce is hot and bubbling.

Makes 4 servings

Autumn Pork Chops

Prep: 10 minutes • **Cook:** 20 minutes

1 tablespoon vegetable oil
4 bone-in pork chops, ½-inch thick (about 2 pounds)
1 can (10¾ ounces) Campbell's® Condensed Cream of Celery Soup (Regular **or** 98% Fat Free)
½ cup apple juice **or** water

2 tablespoons spicy-brown mustard
1 tablespoon honey
Generous dash ground black pepper
Hot cooked medium egg noodles

1. Heat the oil in a 10-inch skillet over medium-high heat. Add the pork and cook until well browned on both sides.

2. Stir the soup, apple juice, mustard, honey and black pepper in the skillet and heat to a boil. Reduce the heat to low. Cover and cook for 5 minutes or until the pork is cooked through. Serve the pork and sauce with the noodles.

Makes 4 servings

Saucy Cranberry Orange Chicken

Prep: 10 minutes • **Cook:** 20 minutes

1 tablespoon vegetable oil
4 skinless, boneless chicken breast
   halves (about 1 pound)
¼ cup orange juice
¼ cup cranberry juice
1 can (10¾ ounces) Campbell's®
   Condensed Cream of Mushroom
   Soup (Regular **or** 98% Fat Free)

1 tablespoon dried cranberries
1 tablespoon chopped fresh sage
   leaves **or** 1 teaspoon ground
   sage
⅛ teaspoon ground black pepper
4 cups hot cooked instant white
   rice
   Sliced green onions (optional)

1. Heat the oil in a 10-inch skillet over medium-high heat. Add the chicken and cook for 10 minutes or until it's well browned on both sides.

2. Add the orange juice, cranberry juice, soup, cranberries, sage and black pepper in the skillet and heat to a boil. Reduce the heat to low. Cover and cook for 5 minutes or until the chicken is cooked through.

3. Serve the chicken mixture over the rice and sprinkle with the onions, if desired.

Makes 4 servings

New Orleans Shrimp Toss

Prep: 15 minutes • **Cook:** 10 minutes

1 pound large shrimp, peeled and deveined
2 tablespoons vegetable oil
2 tablespoons lemon juice
1 tablespoon Worcestershire sauce
1 teaspoon Cajun seasoning
1 medium onion, chopped (about ½ cup)

2 cloves garlic, chopped
1 can (10¾ ounces) Campbell's® Condensed Cream of Chicken with Herbs Soup
½ cup milk
1 teaspoon paprika
2 tablespoons chopped fresh chives
Cornbread **or** biscuits

1. Stir the shrimp, **1 tablespoon** oil, lemon juice, Worcestershire and Cajun seasoning in a medium bowl.

2. Heat the remaining oil in a 10-inch skillet over medium heat. Add the onion and garlic and cook until they're tender.

3. Stir the soup, milk and paprika in the skillet. Heat to a boil. Add the shrimp mixture. Reduce the heat to low. Cover and cook for 5 minutes or until the shrimp turn pink. Garnish with the chives. Serve with cornbread.

Makes 4 servings

Skillet Cheesy Chicken and Rice

Prep: 5 minutes • **Cook:** 20 minutes

1 tablespoon vegetable oil
1½ pounds skinless, boneless chicken breast halves (about 4 to 6)
1 can (10¾ ounces) Campbell's® Condensed Cream of Chicken Soup (Regular **or** 98% Fat Free)
1½ cups water

¼ teaspoon paprika
¼ teaspoon ground black pepper
2 cups fresh **or** frozen broccoli flowerets
1½ cups **uncooked** instant white rice
½ cup shredded Cheddar cheese

1. Heat the oil in a 10-inch skillet over medium-high heat. Add the chicken and cook for 10 minutes or until it's well browned on both sides. Remove the chicken and set aside.

2. Stir in the soup, water, paprika and black pepper. Heat to a boil.

3. Stir in the broccoli and rice. Return the chicken to the skillet and reduce the heat to low. Sprinkle the chicken with additional paprika and black pepper. Top with the cheese. Cover and cook for 5 minutes or until the chicken is cooked through and the rice is tender.

Makes 6 servings

Rosemary Chicken & Mushroom Pasta

Prep: 10 minutes • **Cook:** 20 minutes

2 tablespoons olive **or** vegetable oil
1½ pounds skinless, boneless chicken breast, cut into strips
4 cups sliced mushrooms (about 12 ounces)
1 tablespoon minced garlic

1 tablespoon chopped fresh rosemary leaves **or** 1 teaspoon dried rosemary leaves
1 can (14½ ounces) Campbell's® Chicken Gravy
1 package (16 ounces) linguine **or** spaghetti, cooked and drained
Shredded Parmesan cheese

1. Heat the oil in a 12-inch skillet over medium-high heat. Add the chicken and mushrooms in 2 batches and cook until the chicken is well browned, stirring often. Remove the chicken mixture from the skillet.

2. Reduce the heat to low. Stir the garlic and rosemary in the skillet and cook for 1 minute. Stir the gravy in the skillet and heat to a boil.

3. Return the chicken and mushrooms to the skillet. Cover and cook for 5 minutes or until the chicken is cooked through. Place the pasta in a large serving bowl. Pour the chicken mixture over the pasta. Toss to coat. Serve with the cheese.

Makes 6 servings

Kitchen Tip: For a rustic twist, try whole wheat pasta in the recipe.

Poached Halibut with Pineapple Salsa

Prep: 10 minutes • **Cook:** 15 minutes

1 can (about 15 ounces) pineapple chunks in juice, undrained
1 seedless cucumber, peeled and diced (about 1⅔ cups)
1 medium red pepper, chopped (about ¾ cup)

2 tablespoons chopped red onion
1 teaspoon white wine vinegar
1 teaspoon hot pepper sauce (optional)
1¾ cups Swanson® Chicken Stock
¼ cup white wine
4 halibut fillets (about 1½ pounds)

1. Drain the pineapple and reserve ⅔ **cup** juice.

2. Stir the pineapple chunks, cucumber, red pepper, red onion, vinegar and hot pepper sauce, if desired, in a medium bowl.

3. Heat the stock, wine and reserved pineapple juice in a 12-inch skillet over medium-high heat to a boil. Add the fish to the skillet. Reduce the heat to low. Cover and cook for 10 minutes or until the fish flakes easily when tested with a fork. Serve the fish with the pineapple salsa.

Makes 4 servings

Balsamic Glazed Salmon

Prep: 5 minutes • **Bake:** 15 minutes • **Cook:** 5 minutes

8 **fresh salmon fillets, ¾-inch thick (about 1½ pounds)**
Freshly ground black pepper
3 **tablespoons olive oil**
4½ **teaspoons cornstarch**
1¾ **cups Swanson® Chicken Stock**

3 **tablespoons balsamic vinegar**
1 **tablespoon brown sugar**
1 **tablespoon orange juice**
1 **teaspoon grated orange peel**
Orange slices for garnish

1. Place the salmon in an 11×8-inch (2-quart) shallow baking dish. Sprinkle with black pepper and drizzle with oil. Bake at 350°F. for 15 minutes or until the fish flakes easily when tested with a fork.

2. Stir the cornstarch, stock, vinegar, brown sugar, orange juice and orange peel in a 2-quart saucepan over high heat to a boil. Cook and stir until the mixture boils and thickens.

3. Place the salmon on a serving platter and serve with the sauce. Garnish with the orange slices.

Makes 8 servings

Kitchen Tip: When grating citrus fruits you'll want to avoid rubbing too deeply into the peel. There's a white layer between the outer peel and the flesh, called the pith, which can be bitter.

Monterey Chicken Fajitas

Prep: 15 minutes • **Cook:** 20 minutes

2 tablespoons vegetable oil
4 skinless, boneless chicken breast
  halves (about 1 pound), cut
  into strips
1 medium green pepper, cut into
  2-inch strips (about 1½ cups)
1 medium onion, sliced
  (about ½ cup)

1 can (10¾ ounces) Campbell's®
  Condensed Cream of
  Mushroom Soup (Regular **or**
  98% Fat Free)
½ cup Pace® Picante Sauce
8 flour tortillas (8-inch), warmed
1 cup shredded Monterey Jack
  cheese (about 4 ounces)

1. Heat the oil in a 10-inch skillet over medium-high heat. Add the chicken and cook until it's well browned, stirring often.

2. Reduce the heat to medium. Add the green pepper and onion to the skillet and cook until the vegetables are tender-crisp, stirring occasionally. Stir in the soup and picante sauce and cook until the chicken is cooked through.

3. Spoon **about ½ cup** chicken mixture down the center of **each** tortilla. Top with the cheese and additional picante sauce. Fold the tortillas around the filling.

Makes 8 servings

Tangy Grilled Beef

Prep: 15 minutes • **Grill:** 10 minutes

1 can (10¾ ounces) Campbell's®
  Condensed Tomato Soup
  (Regular **or** Healthy Request®)
2 tablespoons packed brown sugar
2 tablespoons lemon juice
2 tablespoons vegetable oil

1 tablespoon Worcestershire sauce
1 teaspoon garlic powder
¼ teaspoon dried thyme leaves,
  crushed
1½-pound boneless beef sirloin
  steak, ¾-inch thick

1. Stir the soup, brown sugar, lemon juice, oil, Worcestershire, garlic powder and thyme in a medium bowl.

2. Lightly oil the grill rack and heat the grill to medium. Grill the steak for 10 minutes for medium-rare or to desired doneness, turning the steak over once halfway through cooking and brushing often with the soup mixture.

3. Heat the remaining soup mixture in a 1-quart saucepan over medium-high heat to a boil. Slice the steak and serve with the soup mixture.

Makes 6 servings

Kitchen Tip: When you remove the steak from the grill, let it stand for a few minutes before slicing. This "rest" time lets the juices distribute evenly throughout the meat, so they don't all run out when you slice it.

Chicken Scampi

Prep: 10 minutes • **Cook:** 20 minutes

2 tablespoons butter
6 skinless, boneless chicken breast
   halves (about 1½ pounds)
1 can (10¾ ounces) Campbell's®
   Condensed Cream of Chicken
   Soup (Regular **or** 98% Fat Free)

¼ cup water
2 teaspoons lemon juice
2 cloves garlic, minced **or**
   ½ teaspoon garlic powder
Hot cooked pasta

1. Heat the butter in a 10-inch skillet over medium-high heat. Add the chicken and cook for 10 minutes or until well browned on both sides. Remove the chicken from the skillet.

2. Stir the soup, water, lemon juice and garlic in the skillet and heat to a boil. Return the chicken to the skillet. Reduce the heat to low. Cover and cook for 5 minutes or until the chicken is cooked through. Serve the chicken and sauce with the pasta.

Makes 6 servings

Family Favorites

Beef Stroganoff

Prep: 10 minutes • **Cook:** 25 minutes

- **1** tablespoon vegetable oil
- **1** pound boneless beef sirloin steak **or** beef top round steak, ¾-inch thick, cut into thin strips
- **1** medium onion, chopped (about ½ cup)
- **1** can (10¾ ounces) Campbell's® Condensed Cream of Mushroom Soup (Regular **or** 98% Fat Free)
- **½** teaspoon paprika
- **⅓** cup sour cream **or** plain yogurt
- **4** cups hot cooked whole wheat **or** regular egg noodles
  Chopped fresh parsley

1. Heat the oil in a 12-inch nonstick skillet over medium-high heat. Add the beef and cook until it's well browned, stirring often. Remove the beef from the skillet. Pour off any fat.

2. Reduce the heat to medium. Add the onion to the skillet and cook until it's tender.

3. Stir the soup and paprika in the skillet and heat to a boil. Stir in the sour cream. Return the beef to the skillet and cook until the mixture is hot and bubbling. Serve the beef mixture over the noodles. Sprinkle with the parsley.

Makes 4 servings

Slow-Cooked Autumn Brisket

Prep: 20 minutes • **Cook:** 8 hours

1 boneless beef brisket (about
   3 pounds)
1 small head cabbage (about
   1 pound), cut into 8 wedges
1 large sweet potato (about
   ¾ pound), peeled and cut into
   1-inch pieces
1 large onion, cut into 8 wedges

1 medium Granny Smith apple,
   cored and cut into 8 wedges
2 cans (10¾ ounces **each**)
   Campbell's® Condensed Cream
   of Celery Soup (Regular **or** 98%
   Fat Free)
1 cup water
2 teaspoons caraway seed
   (optional)

1. Place the brisket in a 6-quart slow cooker. Top with the cabbage, sweet potato, onion and apple. Stir the soup, water and caraway seed, if desired, in a small bowl. Pour the soup mixture over the brisket and vegetable mixture.

2. Cover and cook on LOW for 8 to 9 hours* or until the brisket is fork-tender. Season as desired.

Or on HIGH for 4 to 5 hours.

Makes 8 servings

Chicken & Stuffing Skillet

Prep: 5 minutes • **Cook:** 25 minutes

1 tablespoon butter	1 can (10¾ ounces) Campbell's®
4 skinless, boneless chicken breast	Condensed Cream of Chicken
halves	Soup (Regular **or** 98% Fat Free)
1 box (6 ounces) Pepperidge Farm®	½ cup milk
One Step Stuffing Chicken Mix	½ cup shredded Cheddar cheese

1. Heat the butter in a 10-inch skillet over medium-high heat. Add the chicken and cook for 15 minutes or until it's well browned on both sides and cooked through. Remove the chicken from the skillet.

2. Prepare the stuffing in the skillet according to the package directions except let stand for 2 minutes.

3. Place the chicken on the stuffing. Stir the soup and milk in a small bowl. Pour the soup mixture over the chicken. Top with the cheese. Cover and cook until the cheese is melted.

Makes 4 servings

Kitchen Tip: Substitute Campbell's® Condensed Cream of Celery **or** Cream of Mushroom Soup for the Cream of Chicken Soup.

Italian Chicken Pasta Salad

Prep: 20 minutes • **Chill:** 30 minutes

3 cups corkscrew-shaped pasta (rotini), cooked and drained

2 cans (4.5 ounces **each**) Swanson® Premium Chunk Chicken Breast in Water, drained

1 large zucchini, cut in half lengthwise and sliced (about 1½ cups)

1 cup sliced mushrooms (about 3 ounces)

1 cup cherry tomatoes, cut in quarters

¾ cup creamy fat-free Italian herb dressing

Stir the pasta, chicken, zucchini, mushrooms, tomatoes and dressing in a large bowl until coated. Cover and refrigerate for 30 minutes.

Makes 4 servings

Cranberry Dijon Pork Chops

Prep: 10 minutes • **Bake:** 45 minutes

1 tablespoon olive oil
4 boneless pork chops, 1-inch thick (about 1¼ pounds)
1 can (10¾ ounces) Campbell's® Condensed Cream of Celery Soup (Regular **or** 98% Fat Free)

½ cup cranberry juice
2 tablespoons Dijon-style mustard
¼ teaspoon dried thyme leaves, crushed
¼ cup dried cranberries **or** cherries
Hot cooked noodles

1. Heat the oil in a 10-inch oven-safe skillet over medium-high heat. Add the pork chops and cook until the chops are well browned on both sides. Remove the pork chops and set them aside.

2. Stir in the soup, cranberry juice, mustard and thyme. Heat to a boil. Return the pork chops to the skillet and cover.

3. Bake at 350°F. for 45 minutes or until chops are cooked through but slightly pink in center. Place the pork chops on a serving plate. Stir the cranberries into the skillet. Serve the sauce with the pork and noodles.

Makes 4 servings

Moroccan Lamb Stew

Prep: 15 minutes • **Cook:** 1 hour 35 minutes

2 pounds lamb for stew, cut into
  1-inch pieces
½ teaspoon ground cinnamon
¼ teaspoon ground cloves
¼ teaspoon ground black pepper
1 tablespoon olive oil
1 large onion, chopped (about 1 cup)

4 cups Swanson® Chicken Stock
1 cup dried lentils
2 medium potatoes, cut into cubes
  (about 2 cups)
  Hot cooked couscous
  Chopped fresh cilantro leaves
  Chopped tomatoes

1. Season the lamb with the cinnamon, cloves and black pepper.

2. Heat the oil in an 8-quart saucepot over medium-high heat. Add the lamb
in 2 batches and cook until it's well browned, stirring often. Remove the lamb
from the saucepot.

3. Reduce the heat to medium. Add the onion to the saucepot and cook until
it's tender-crisp. Return the lamb to the saucepot. Stir in the stock and heat to a
boil. Reduce the heat to low. Cover and cook for 1 hour.

4. Stir in the lentils and potatoes. Cook for 20 minutes or until the lamb
is cooked through and the lentils and potatoes are tender. Serve over the
couscous and sprinkle with the cilantro, if desired. Top with tomatoes.

Makes 8 servings

Broccoli and Pasta Bianco

Prep: 20 minutes • **Bake:** 25 minutes

1 package (1 pound) medium tube-shaped pasta (penne **or** ziti) (about 6 cups)

4 cups fresh **or** frozen broccoli flowerets

1 can (10¾ ounces) Campbell's® Condensed Cream of Mushroom Soup (Regular **or** 98% Fat Free)

1½ cups milk

½ teaspoon ground black pepper

1½ cups shredded mozzarella cheese (about 6 ounces)

¼ cup shredded Parmesan cheese

1. Heat the oven to 350°F.

2. Cook the pasta according to the package directions. Add the broccoli for the last 4 minutes of cooking time. Drain the pasta and broccoli well in a colander.

3. Stir the soup, milk and black pepper in a 2-quart shallow baking dish. Stir in the pasta mixture, ¾ **cup** mozzarella cheese and **2 tablespoons** Parmesan cheese. Top with the remaining mozzarella and Parmesan cheeses.

4. Bake for 25 minutes or until the pasta mixture is hot and bubbling and the cheese is melted.

Makes 8 servings

Kitchen Tip: Creamy white pastas like this one taste great with the tang and heat of crushed red pepper flakes. Serve it on the side.

Baked Chicken & Cheese Risotto

Prep: 10 minutes • **Bake:** 45 minutes • **Stand:** 5 minutes

1 can (10¾ ounces) Campbell's® Condensed Cream of Mushroom Soup (Regular **or** 98% Fat Free)

1¼ cups water

½ cup milk

¼ cup shredded part-skim mozzarella cheese

3 tablespoons grated Parmesan cheese

1½ cups frozen mixed vegetables

2 skinless, boneless chicken breast halves (about ½ pound), cut into cubes

¾ cup **uncooked** Arborio **or** regular long-grain white rice

1. Stir the soup, water, milk, mozzarella cheese, Parmesan cheese, vegetables, chicken and rice in a 3-quart shallow baking dish. Cover the baking dish.

2. Bake at 400°F. for 35 minutes. Stir the rice mixture. Cover the baking dish.

3. Bake for 10 minutes or until the chicken is cooked through and the rice is tender. Let stand, covered, for 5 minutes.

Makes 4 servings

Barbecued Pork Spareribs

Prep: 15 minutes • **Cook:** 35 minutes • **Grill:** 10 minutes

4 **pounds pork spareribs, cut into serving-sized pieces**
1 **can (10¼ ounces) Campbell's® Beef Gravy**

¾ **cup barbecue sauce**
2 **tablespoons packed brown sugar**

1. Place the ribs into an 8-quart saucepot and add water to cover. Heat over medium-high heat to a boil. Reduce the heat to low. Cover and cook for 30 minutes or until the meat is tender. Drain the ribs well in a colander.

2. Stir the gravy, barbecue sauce and brown sugar in a large bowl. Add the ribs and toss to coat.

3. Lightly oil the grill rack and heat the grill to medium-high. Grill the ribs for 10 minutes, turning and brushing occasionally with the gravy mixture, until the ribs are well glazed.

Makes 4 servings

Kitchen Tip: Use the gravy mixture as a basting sauce when grilling chicken.

Fish & Vegetable Skillet

Prep: 15 minutes • **Cook:** 15 minutes

¼ cup water
2 tablespoons dry white wine (optional)
½ teaspoon dried thyme leaves, crushed
 Generous dash ground black pepper
1 large carrot, cut into matchstick-thin strips (about 1 cup)
2 stalks celery, cut into matchstick-thin strips (about 1⅓ cups)

1 small onion, chopped (about ¼ cup)
1 can (10¾ ounces) Campbell's® Condensed Cream of Mushroom Soup (Regular, 98% Fat Free **or** Healthy Request®)
4 firm white fish fillets (cod, haddock **or** halibut) (about 1 pound)

1. Heat the water, wine, thyme, black pepper, carrot, celery and onion in a 10-inch skillet over medium-high heat to a boil. Reduce the heat to low. Cover and cook for 5 minutes or until the vegetables are tender-crisp.

2. Stir the soup in the skillet. Top with the fish. Cover and cook for 5 minutes or until the fish flakes easily when tested with a fork.

Makes 4 servings

Sirloin Steak Olé

Prep: 5 minutes • **Grill:** 20 minutes • **Stand:** 10 minutes

1 boneless beef sirloin steak **or top round steak, 1½-inches thick (about 1½ pounds)**

1 jar (16 ounces) Pace® Picante Sauce

1. Lightly oil the grill rack and heat the grill to medium. Grill the steak for 20 minutes for medium-rare or to desired doneness, turning the steak over halfway through grilling and brushing often with **1 cup** picante sauce.

2. Let stand for 10 minutes before slicing. Serve with additional picante sauce.

Makes 6 servings

Sausage-Stuffed Green Peppers

Prep: 20 minutes • **Bake:** 40 minutes

1 tablespoon vegetable oil
1 pound sweet Italian pork sausage, casing removed
1 medium onion, chopped (about ½ cup)
1 teaspoon dried oregano leaves, crushed

1 cup shredded part-skim mozzarella cheese (about 4 ounces)
4 medium green peppers, seeded and cut in half lengthwise
2 cups Prego® Traditional Italian Sauce **or** Tomato, Basil & Garlic Italian Sauce

1. Heat the oven to 400°F. Heat the oil in a 10-inch skillet over medium-high heat. Add the sausage and cook until it's well browned, stirring often to separate the meat. Add the onion and oregano and cook until the onion is tender. Pour off any fat. Stir in the cheese.

2. Arrange the peppers in a 3-quart shallow baking dish. Spoon the sausage mixture into the peppers. Pour the Italian sauce over the filled peppers. Cover the baking dish.

3. Bake for 40 minutes or until the peppers are tender.

Makes 8 servings

Chicken Broccoli Divan

Prep: 10 minutes • **Bake:** 20 minutes

4 cups cooked broccoli flowerets
1½ cups cubed cooked chicken
1 can (10¾ ounces) Campbell's®
  Condensed Cream of Chicken
  Soup (Regular **or** 98% Fat-Free)

⅓ cup milk
½ cup shredded Cheddar cheese
2 tablespoons dry bread crumbs
1 tablespoon butter, melted

1. Place the broccoli and chicken into a 9-inch pie plate.

2. Stir the soup and milk in a small bowl. Pour the soup mixture over the broccoli and chicken. Sprinkle with the cheese. Stir the bread crumbs and butter in a small bowl. Sprinkle the bread crumb mixture over the cheese.

3. Bake at 350°F. for 20 minutes or until the chicken is hot and bubbling.

Makes 4 servings

Creamy 3-Cheese Pasta

Prep: 20 minutes • **Bake:** 20 minutes

1 can (10¾ ounces) Campbell's®
Condensed Cream of Mushroom
Soup (Regular **or** 98% Fat Free)
1 cup milk
¼ teaspoon ground black pepper

1 package (8 ounces) shredded
two-cheese blend
⅓ cup grated Parmesan cheese
3 cups corkscrew-shaped pasta
(rotelle), cooked and drained

1. Stir the soup, milk, black pepper and cheeses in a 1½-quart casserole dish. Stir in the pasta.

2. Bake at 400°F. for 20 minutes or until hot.

3. Stir before serving.

Makes 4 servings

Pan-Seared Beef Steaks with Garlic Red Wine Gravy

Prep: 10 minutes • **Cook:** 15 minutes

3 teaspoons butter
8 (5 ounces **each**) beef filet
   mignons, ¾-inch thick
½ cup chopped shallots **or** onion
1 clove garlic, minced

1 can (10¼ ounces) Campbell's®
   Beef Gravy
½ cup Burgundy **or** other dry red
   wine
   Fresh chives, sliced

1. Heat **1 teaspoon** butter in a 12-inch skillet over medium-high heat. Add the beef in 2 batches and cook for 8 minutes for medium or to desired doneness, turning the beef over once and adding an additional **1 teaspoon** butter as needed during cooking. Remove the beef from the skillet and keep warm.

2. Reduce the heat to medium. Add the remaining butter to the skillet. Add the shallots and cook for 1 minute. Add the garlic and cook for 30 seconds.

3. Stir in the gravy and wine and heat to a boil. Return the steaks to the skillet and cook until they're heated through. Serve with chives.

Makes 8 servings

Kitchen Tip: Try using other red wines instead of the Burgundy, such as Cabernet Sauvignon, Merlot **or** Pinot Noir.

Cheesy Chicken & Rice Casserole

Prep: 15 minutes • **Bake:** 50 minutes • **Stand:** 10 minutes

1 can (10¾ ounces) Campbell's®
Condensed Cream of Chicken
Soup (Regular, 98% Fat Free **or**
Healthy Request®)
1⅓ cups water
¾ cup **uncooked** regular long-grain
white rice

½ teaspoon onion powder
¼ teaspoon ground black pepper
2 cups frozen mixed vegetables
4 skinless, boneless chicken breast
halves (about 1 pound)
½ cup shredded Cheddar cheese

1. Heat the oven to 375°F. Stir the soup, water, rice, onion powder, black pepper and vegetables in a 2-quart shallow baking dish.

2. Top with the chicken. Cover the baking dish.

3. Bake for 50 minutes or until the chicken is cooked through and the rice is tender. Top with the cheese. Let the casserole stand for 10 minutes. Stir the rice before serving.

Makes 4 servings

Kitchen Tip: To Make Alfredo: Substitute broccoli flowerets for the vegetables and substitute ¼ **cup** grated Parmesan for the Cheddar cheese. Add **2 tablespoons** Parmesan cheese with the soup. Sprinkle the chicken with the remaining Parmesan cheese.

Lower Fat: Use Campbell's® 98% Fat Free Cream of Chicken Soup instead of regular soup and use lowfat cheese instead of regular cheese.

Mexican: In place of the onion powder and black pepper use **1 teaspoon** chili powder. Substitute Mexican cheese blend for the Cheddar.

Italian: In place of the onion powder and black pepper use **1 teaspoon** Italian seasoning, crushed. Substitute ⅓ **cup** shredded Parmesan for the Cheddar.

Chicken Nacho Tacos

Prep: 15 minutes • **Cook:** 10 minutes

1 tablespoon vegetable oil
1 medium onion, chopped
(about ½ cup)
½ teaspoon chili powder
1 can (10¾ ounces) Campbell's®
Condensed Fiesta Nacho
Cheese Soup

2 cans (4.5 ounces **each**) Swanson®
Premium White Chunk Chicken
Breast in Water, drained
8 taco shells, warmed
Shredded lettuce
Chopped tomato

1. Heat the oil in a 10-inch skillet over medium-high heat. Add the onion and chili powder and cook until the onion is tender, stirring often.

2. Stir the soup and chicken in the skillet and cook until the mixture is hot and bubbling. Spoon the chicken mixture into the taco shells. Top with the lettuce and tomato.

Makes 4 servings

Holiday Fun

German Potato Salad

Prep: 15 minutes • **Cook:** 30 minutes

- 10 medium potatoes
- 1¾ Swanson® Beef Broth (Regular, Lower Sodium **or** Certified Organic)
- ¼ cup cider vinegar
- ¼ cup all-purpose flour
- 3 tablespoons sugar
- ½ teaspoon celery seed
- ⅛ teaspoon ground black pepper
- 1 medium onion, chopped (about ½ cup)
- 3 tablespoons chopped fresh parsley

1. Place the potatoes into a 4-quart saucepan. Add water to cover. Heat over high heat to a boil. Reduce the heat to low. Cook for 20 minutes or until the potatoes are tender. Drain. Let cool and cut in cubes. Place the potatoes into a large bowl.

2. Stir the broth, vinegar, flour, sugar, celery seed and black pepper in the saucepan. Stir in the onion. Cook and stir over medium-high heat until the mixture boils and thickens. Reduce the heat to low. Cook for 5 minutes or until the onion is tender.

3. Add the parsley and broth mixture to the potatoes and stir to coat. Serve warm.

Makes 12 serving

Kitchen Tip: You can let this dish stand for a few minutes before serving. The dressing will soak into the warm potatoes—delicious!

Green Bean Casserole

Prep: 10 minutes • **Bake:** 30 minutes

1 can (10¾ ounces) Campbell's®
   Condensed Cream of
   Mushroom Soup (Regular **or**
   98% Fat Free)
½ cup milk
1 teaspoon soy sauce

Dash ground black pepper
2 packages (10 ounces **each**)
   frozen cut green beans, cooked
   and drained
1 can (2.8 ounces) French fried
   onions (1⅓ cups)

1. Stir the soup, milk, soy sauce, black pepper, green beans and ⅔ **cup** onions in a 1½-quart casserole.

2. Bake at 350°F. for 25 minutes or until hot. Stir the green bean mixture.

3. Sprinkle the remaining onions over the green bean mixture. Bake for 5 minutes more or until onions are golden brown.

Makes 5 servings

Kitchen Tip: You can also make this classic side dish with fresh **or** canned green beans. You will need either **1½ pounds** fresh green beans, cut into 1-inch pieces, cooked and drained **or 2 cans** (about 16 ounces **each**) cut green beans, drained for the frozen green beans.

Roasted Asparagus with Lemon & Goat Cheese

Prep: 10 minutes • **Cook:** 20 minutes

Vegetable cooking spray
2 pounds asparagus, trimmed
1 tablespoon olive oil
Freshly ground black pepper
½ cup Swanson® Vegetable Broth
(Regular **or** Certified Organic)

3 ounces soft goat cheese,
crumbled
1 tablespoon lemon juice
1 teaspoon grated lemon peel

1. Heat the oven to 425°F. Spray a 17×11-inch roasting pan or shallow baking sheet with the cooking spray.

2. Stir the asparagus and oil in the pan. Season with the black pepper. Pour in the broth.

3. Roast the asparagus for 20 minutes or until it's tender, stirring once during cooking. Top with the cheese, lemon juice and lemon peel.

Makes 6 servings

Longevity Noodle Soup

Prep: 20 minutes · **Cook:** 15 minutes

4 teaspoons cornstarch
2 tablespoons water
1 tablespoon sesame oil
8 cups Swanson® Chicken Broth
   (Regular, Natural Goodness® or
   Certified Organic)
3 tablespoons soy sauce
2 eggs, beaten

1 package (1 pound) thin
   spaghetti, cooked and drained
   (about 8 cups)
¼ pound sliced cooked ham,
   cut into 2-inch-long strips
   (about 1 cup)
4 medium green onions, chopped
   (about ½ cup)

1. Stir the cornstarch, water and sesame oil in a small bowl until the mixture is smooth.

2. Heat the broth and soy sauce in a 3-quart saucepan over medium heat to a boil. Stir the cornstarch mixture in the saucepan. Cook and stir until the mixture boils and thickens.

3. Reduce the heat to low. Gradually stir the eggs into the saucepan. Remove the saucepan from the heat. Divide the spaghetti, ham and green onions among **8** serving bowls. Spoon **about 1 cup** broth mixture into **each**. Serve immediately.

Makes 8 servings

Cheesy Mexican Cornbread

Prep: 15 minutes • **Bake:** 20 minutes • **Cool:** 15 minutes

3 tablespoons butter, melted
1 cup yellow cornmeal
¾ cup all-purpose flour
⅓ cup sugar
1 tablespoon baking powder
1 can (10¾ ounces) Campbell's®
   Condensed Cheddar Cheese Soup

½ cup milk
1 egg, beaten
1 can (about 8 ounces) whole
   kernel corn, drained
½ cup shredded Cheddar cheese
   (2 ounces)

1. Heat the oven to 450°F. Pour **1 tablespoon** melted butter into a 9-inch round cake pan. Set aside.

2. Mix the cornmeal, flour, sugar and baking powder in a 2-quart bowl. Beat the soup, milk, egg and remaining melted butter in a 1-quart bowl with fork or whisk until the ingredients are mixed. Stir the soup mixture into cornmeal mixture with a fork just until the dry ingredients are moistened. Stir in the corn. Pour the batter into the prepared pan.

3. Bake for 20 minutes or until a toothpick inserted in the center of the bread comes out clean. Remove the pan from the oven and place on wire rack. Sprinkle with the cheese. Let cool for 15 minutes. Cut into **8** wedges. Serve warm.

Makes 8 servings

Kitchen Tip: Substitute **1 cup** frozen whole kernel corn, thawed, for the canned corn.

Holiday Potato Pancakes

Prep: 25 minutes · **Cook:** 30 minutes

8 medium all-purpose potatoes (about 3 pounds), peeled and grated (about 7 cups)

2 cans (10¾ ounces **each**) Campbell's® Condensed Broccoli Cheese Soup (Regular **or** 98% Fat Free)

3 eggs, beaten

2 tablespoons all-purpose flour

¼ teaspoon freshly ground black pepper

½ cup vegetable oil

Sour cream

Chopped chives

1. Wrap the grated potatoes in a clean dish or paper towel. Twist the towel and squeeze to wring out as much of the liquid as possible.

2. Mix the soup, eggs, flour, black pepper and potatoes in a 3-quart bowl.

3. Heat ¼ **cup** oil in a deep nonstick 12-inch skillet over medium-high heat. Drop a scant ¼ **cup** potato mixture into the pan, making **4** pancakes at a time. Press on **each** pancake to flatten to 3 or 4 inches. Cook 4 minutes, turning once or until pancakes are dark golden brown. Remove the pancakes and keep warm. Repeat with the remaining potato mixture, adding more of the remaining oil as needed. Serve with the sour cream and chives.

Makes 36 pancakes

Eggplant Tomato Gratin

Prep: 20 minutes • **Bake:** 45 minutes • **Stand:** 10 minutes

Vegetable cooking spray
1 large eggplant (about
  1¼ pounds) cut into ½-inch-
  thick slices
1 can (10¾ ounces) Campbell's®
  Condensed Cream of Celery
  Soup (Regular **or** 98% Fat Free)
½ cup milk
¼ cup grated Parmesan cheese

2 large tomatoes, cut into ½-inch-
  thick slices (about 2 cups)
1 medium onion, thinly sliced
  (about ½ cup)
¼ cup chopped fresh basil leaves
¼ cup Italian-seasoned dry bread
  crumbs
1 tablespoon chopped fresh
  parsley (optional)
1 tablespoon olive oil

1. Heat the oven to 425°F. Spray a baking sheet with cooking spray. Arrange the eggplant in a single layer. Bake for 20 minutes or until tender, turning halfway through baking. Spray 3-quart shallow baking dish with cooking spray.

2. Stir the soup, milk and cheese in a small bowl.

3. Layer **half** the eggplant, tomatoes, onion, basil and soup mixture in the prepared dish. Repeat the layers.

4. Stir the bread crumbs, parsley and oil in a small bowl. Sprinkle over the soup mixture.

5. Reduce the heat to 400°F. and bake for 25 minutes or until hot and golden brown. Let stand for 10 minutes.

Makes 8 servings

Kitchen Tip: Prepare ahead up to topping with the bread crumb mixture. Cover and refrigerate overnight. Add the bread crumb mixture and bake at 400°F. for 30 minutes or until hot and golden brown.

Herb Roasted Turkey

Prep: 15 minutes • **Cook:** 4 hours 20 minutes • **Stand:** 10 minutes

1¾ cups Swanson® Chicken Stock
3 tablespoons lemon juice
1 teaspoon dried basil leaves, crushed
1 teaspoon dried thyme leaves, crushed

⅛ teaspoon ground black pepper
1 (12- to 14-pound) turkey
2 cans (14½ ounces **each**) Campbell's® Turkey Gravy

1. Stir the stock, lemon juice, basil, thyme and black pepper in a small bowl.

2. Roast the turkey according to the package directions, basting occasionally with the stock mixture during cooking. Let the turkey stand for 10 minutes before slicing. Discard any remaining stock mixture.

3. Heat the gravy in a 1-quart saucepan over medium heat until it's hot and bubbling. Serve with the turkey.

Makes 12 servings

Heavenly Sweet Potatoes

Prep: 10 minutes • **Bake:** 20 minutes

Vegetable cooking spray
1 can (40 ounces) cut sweet
   potatoes in heavy syrup,
   drained
¼ teaspoon ground cinnamon

⅛ teaspoon ground ginger
¾ cup Swanson® Chicken Broth
   (Regular, Natural Goodness® **or**
   Certified Organic)
2 cups miniature marshmallows

1. Heat the oven to 350°F.

2. Spray a 1½-quart casserole with cooking spray.

3. Put the potatoes, cinnamon and ginger in an electric mixer bowl. Beat at medium speed until almost smooth. Add the broth and beat until potatoes are fluffy. Spoon the potato mixture in the prepared dish. Top with the marshmallows.

4. Bake for 20 minutes or until heated through and marshmallows are golden brown.

Makes 8 servings

Pumpkin Apple Mash

Prep: 10 minutes • **Cook:** 20 minutes

2 tablespoons butter
1 small onion, chopped (about ¼ cup)
¾ cup Swanson® Chicken Broth (Regular, Natural Goodness® or Certified Organic)
1 tablespoon packed brown sugar
¼ teaspoon dried thyme leaves, crushed

⅛ teaspoon ground black pepper
1 pumpkin **or** calabaza squash (about 2½ pounds), peeled, seeded and cut into 1-inch pieces (about 5 to 6 cups)
2 medium McIntosh apples, peeled, cored and cut into 1-inch pieces

1. Heat the butter in a 4-quart saucepan over medium-high heat. Add the onion and cook until the onion is tender-crisp.

2. Stir the broth, brown sugar, thyme, black pepper and pumpkin in the saucepan and heat to a boil. Reduce the heat to low. Cover and cook for 10 minutes or until the pumpkin is tender.

3. Stir the apples in the saucepan. Cook for 5 minutes or until the apples are tender. Mash the pumpkin mixture, adding additional broth, if needed, until desired consistency.

Makes 4 servings

Layered Cranberry Walnut Stuffing

Prep: 10 minutes • **Bake:** 25 minutes

2 boxes (6 ounces **each**)
 Pepperidge Farm® Stuffing Mix
1½ cups Swanson® Chicken Broth
 (Regular, Natural Goodness® **or**
 Certified Organic)

2 tablespoons butter
1 can (16 ounces) whole cranberry
 sauce
½ cup walnuts, toasted and
 chopped

1. Prepare the stuffing using the broth and butter according to the package directions.

2. Spoon **half** of the stuffing into a 2-quart casserole. Spoon **half** of the cranberry sauce over the stuffing. Sprinkle with ¼ **cup** walnuts. Repeat the layers.

3. Bake at 350°F. for 25 minutes or until hot.

Makes 6 servings

Kitchen Tip: The flavor and crispness of nuts come out when they're toasted, and the nuts are easier to chop when warm. Spread the nuts in a single layer on a baking sheet, then bake them in a preheated 350°F. oven for 10 minutes or until they're golden brown. Stir them occasionally so they toast evenly.

Lemon Herb Broccoli Casserole

Prep: 10 minutes • **Bake:** 30 minutes

1 can (10¾ ounces) Campbell's®
   Condensed Cream of Chicken
   with Herbs Soup
½ cup milk

1 tablespoon lemon juice
4 cups frozen broccoli cuts, thawed
1 can (2.8 ounces) French fried
   onions (1⅓ cups)

1. Stir the soup, milk, lemon juice, broccoli and ⅔ **cup** onions in a 1½-quart casserole. Cover the casserole.

2. Bake at 350°F. for 25 minutes or until the broccoli is tender. Stir the broccoli mixture. Sprinkle with the remaining onions.

3. Bake for 5 minutes more or until the onions are golden brown.

Makes 6 servings

Kitchen Tip: To thaw the broccoli, microwave on HIGH for 3 minutes.

Swiss Vegetable Casserole

Prep: 5 minutes • **Bake:** 45 minutes

1 can (10¾ ounces) Campbell's®
  Condensed Cream of
  Mushroom Soup (Regular **or**
  98% Fat Free)
⅓ cup sour cream
¼ teaspoon ground black pepper

1 bag (16 ounces) frozen vegetable
  combination (broccoli,
  cauliflower, carrots), thawed
1 can (2.8 ounces) French fried
  onions (1⅓ cups)
½ cup shredded Swiss cheese

1. Stir the soup, sour cream, black pepper, vegetables, ⅔ **cup** onions and ¼ **cup** cheese in a 2-quart casserole. Cover the casserole.

2. Bake at 350°F. for 40 minutes or until the vegetables are tender. Stir the vegetable mixture. Top with the remaining onions and cheese.

3. Bake for 5 minutes or until the cheese is melted.

Makes 4 servings

Kitchen Tip: If you like, stir **1 jar** (4 ounces) chopped pimientos, drained, into the vegetable mixture before baking.

For Cheddar Cheese Lovers: Use Cheddar cheese instead of Swiss cheese.

Loaded Baked Potato Casserole

Prep: 15 minutes • **Bake:** 35 minutes

1 bag (32 ounces) frozen Southern-style hash brown potatoes, thawed (about 7½ cups)
1 can (6 ounces) French fried onions (2⅔ cups)
1 cup frozen peas, thawed
1 cup shredded Cheddar cheese (4 ounces)

4 slices bacon, cooked and crumbled
2 cans (10¾ ounces **each**) Campbell's® Condensed Cream of Celery Soup (Regular **or** 98% Fat Free)
1 cup milk

1. Stir the potatoes, **1⅓ cups** onions, peas, cheese and bacon in a 13×9×2-inch shallow baking dish.

2. Mix the soup and milk and pour over the potato mixture. Cover the dish.

3. Bake at 350°F. for 30 minutes or until hot. Stir the potato mixture.

4. Sprinkle with the remaining onions. Bake for 5 minutes more or until onions are golden brown.

Makes 8 servings

Kitchen Tip: To thaw the hash browns, cut off one corner of bag and microwave on HIGH for 5 minutes.

Scalloped Apple Bake

Prep: 25 minutes • **Bake:** 40 minutes

4 tablespoons butter, melted	**½** cup pecan halves, coarsely chopped
¼ cup sugar	**1** can (16 ounces) whole berry cranberry sauce
2 teaspoons grated orange peel	**⅓** cup orange juice **or** water
1 teaspoon ground cinnamon	**4** large cooking apples, cored and thinly sliced (about 6 cups)
1½ cups Pepperidge Farm® Corn Bread Stuffing	

1. Mix the butter, sugar, orange peel, cinnamon, stuffing and pecans in a 1-quart bowl. Set the mixture aside.

2. Mix the cranberry sauce, juice and apples in a 3-quart bowl. Add **half** of the stuffing mixture and stir lightly to coat. Spoon into an 8-inch square baking dish. Sprinkle the remaining stuffing mixture over the apple mixture.

3. Bake at 375°F. for 40 minutes or until the apples are tender.

Makes 6 servings

Bloody Fingers

Prep: 15 minutes • **Bake:** 5 minutes

24 sliced blanched almonds
  Red liquid **or** paste food coloring
 2 packages (about 9 ounces **each**)
  refrigerated fully cooked breaded
  chicken strips (about 24)

1 egg, slightly beaten
1 jar (24 ounces) Prego®
  Traditional Italian Sauce

1. Heat the oven to 400°F. Brush the almonds with the food coloring to coat. Set them aside to dry for about 10 minutes.

2. Place the chicken strips on a baking sheet. Brush the narrow end of the chicken strips with egg and press almonds on the egg wash to attach. Bake for 5 minutes or until hot.

3. Pour the Italian sauce in a 2-quart saucepan over medium heat. Cook until it's hot and bubbling, stirring occasionally. Arrange the chicken on a serving platter. Serve with the sauce for dipping.

Makes 8 servings

Kitchen Tip: Substitute frozen fully cooked breaded chicken strips for the refrigerated chicken strips. Increase the bake time to 10 minutes.

Pizza Fondue

Prep: 10 minutes · **Cook:** 10 minutes

½ cup finely chopped pepperoni
1 small green **or** red pepper, chopped (about ½ cup)
½ of an 8-ounce package cream cheese, cut into cubes

⅓ cup grated Parmesan cheese
1½ cups Prego® Traditional Italian Sauce
Italian bread cubes **or** tortilla chips

1. Cook the pepperoni and green pepper in a 2-quart saucepan over medium heat for 4 minutes or until the pepper is tender.

2. Stir in the cream cheese and Parmesan cheese. Cook and stir until the cheese is melted. Stir in the Italian sauce and cook until the mixture is heated through. Serve with the bread cubes for dipping.

Makes 3 cups

Goblin's Toes

Thaw: 40 minutes · **Prep:** 10 minutes · **Bake:** 20 minutes

½ of a 17.3-ounce package
Pepperidge Farm® Frozen Puff
Pastry Sheets (1 sheet)

1 package (14 ounces) cocktail
franks (about 30)
¼ cup prepared mustard
¼ cup ketchup

1. Thaw the pastry sheet at room temperature for 40 minutes or until it's easy to handle. Heat the oven to 375°F. Lightly grease a baking sheet.

2. Unfold the pastry sheet on a lightly floured surface. Cut it in half lengthwise. Cut **each** half crosswise into **15** (½-inch-wide) strips. Wrap one end of **each** cocktail frank with **1** pastry strip, overlapping slightly to resemble a "bandage." Put them on the baking sheet about 1 inch apart.

3. Bake for 20 minutes or until the pastry is golden. Remove the cocktail franks from the baking sheet and cool them slightly on a wire rack. Dollop some mustard on the toes. Serve with remaining mustard and ketchup for dipping.

Makes 30 appetizers

October Dinner Fondue

Prep: 15 minutes • **Cook:** 15 minutes

1 **can (10¾ ounces) Campbell's®
Condensed Cream of Chicken
Soup (Regular or 98% Fat Free)**
¾ **cup milk**
½ **teaspoon chili powder**
½ **teaspoon ground cumin**
1 **cup shredded Cheddar cheese
(about 4 ounces)**

2 **tablespoons chopped fresh
cilantro leaves**

Assorted Dippers: Cooked breaded
chicken breast tenders, cooked shrimp,
tortellini, mini ravioli, French fries,
steamed fresh vegetables (cauliflower,
broccoli, green beans **or** zucchini)

1. Heat the soup and milk in a 2-quart saucepan over medium heat until the
mixture is hot and bubbling, stirring occasionally. Stir in the chili powder,
cumin and cheese. Cook and stir until the cheese melts. Stir in the cilantro.

2. Pour the soup mixture into a fondue pot.

3. Serve warm with the *Assorted Dippers*.

Makes 2 cups

Kitchen Tip: Try serving in
a real pumpkin! Carefully
slice off the top third of a
small pumpkin. Scoop out
the seeds and scrape away
all of the stringy fibers.
Cover with a damp paper
towel. Microwave on HIGH
for 30 seconds at a time,
until slightly warm. Pour in
the soup mixture and serve
immediately.

Vegetables & Sides

Crab and Asparagus Risotto

Prep: 15 minutes • **Cook:** 25 minutes • **Stand:** 5 minutes

- 2 tablespoons olive oil
- 1 medium orange pepper, diced (about 1 cup)
- ½ cup chopped onion **or** shallots
- 2 cups **uncooked** Arborio rice **or** regular long-grain white rice
- ½ cup dry white wine
- 6 cups Swanson® Chicken Broth (Regular, Natural Goodness® **or** Certified Organic)
- ½ pound asparagus **or** green beans
- ½ pound refrigerated pasteurized crabmeat (about 1½ cups)
- ¼ cup grated Parmesan cheese

1. Heat the oil in a 4-quart saucepan over medium heat. Add the pepper and onion and cook for 3 minutes or until the vegetables are tender.

2. Add the rice to the saucepan and cook and stir for 2 minutes. Add the wine and cook and stir until it's absorbed. Add **2 cups** of the broth and cook and stir until it's absorbed. Add the remaining broth, ½ **cup** at a time, stirring until the broth is absorbed before adding more. Stir in the asparagus and crabmeat with the last broth addition.

3. Stir in the cheese. Remove the saucepan from the heat. Cover and let stand for 5 minutes. Serve the risotto with additional cheese, if desired.

Makes 8 servings

Kitchen Tip: If you have some light or heavy cream on hand, stir in 2 tablespoons with the Parmesan cheese for a creamier dish.

Glazed Snow Peas and Carrots

Prep: 15 minutes • **Cook:** 10 minutes

4 teaspoons cornstarch	**1 medium onion, chopped**
1¾ cups Swanson® Vegetable Broth	**(about ½ cup)**
(Regular or Certified Organic)	**¾ pound snow peas**
4 medium carrots, sliced (about 2 cups)	**1 teaspoon lemon juice**

1. Stir the cornstarch and **1 cup** of the broth in a small bowl until the mixture is smooth and set it aside.

2. Heat the remaining broth in a 10-inch skillet over medium-high heat to a boil. Add the carrots and onion.

3. Reduce the heat to low. Cook for 5 minutes or until the carrots are tender-crisp. Add the snow peas and cook for 2 minutes.

4. Stir the cornstarch mixture and add it to the skillet. Cook until the mixture boils and thickens, stirring constantly. Stir in the lemon juice.

Makes 8 servings

Mediterranean Chop Salad

Prep: 25 minutes

3 stalks celery, sliced (about 1½ cups) **or** 1 cup sliced fennel

1 cup chopped roasted red **or** yellow pepper

1 large seedless cucumber, peeled and chopped (about 1⅔ cups)

½ cup chopped pitted ripe olives

½ cup prepared balsamic vinaigrette salad dressing

1 package (12 ounces) hearts of romaine, chopped (about 8 cups)

1 box (5.5 ounces) Pepperidge Farm® Seasoned Croutons (your favorite variety)

Freshly ground black pepper

Parmesan cheese shavings

1. Stir the celery, peppers, cucumber, olives and dressing in a large serving bowl. Cover and refrigerate until serving time.

2. Add the lettuce and croutons to the dressing mixture just before serving and toss to coat. Season with the black pepper. Top with the cheese.

Makes 8 servings

Toasted Corn & Sage Harvest Risotto

Prep: 15 minutes • **Cook:** 35 minutes

1 tablespoon olive oil
1 cup fresh **or** drained canned whole kernel corn
1 large orange **or** red pepper, chopped (about 1 cup)
1 medium onion, chopped (about ½ cup)
1¾ cups **uncooked** regular long-grain white rice

4 cups Swanson® Chicken Broth (Regular, Natural Goodness® **or** Certified Organic)
1 teaspoon ground sage
1 can (10¾ ounces) Campbell's® Condensed Cream of Celery Soup (Regular **or** 98% Fat Free)
¼ cup grated Parmesan cheese

1. Heat the oil in a 4-quart saucepan over medium heat. Add the corn, pepper and onion and cook for 5 minutes or until the vegetables are lightly browned.

2. Add the rice to the saucepan and cook and stir for 30 seconds. Stir in the broth and sage and heat to a boil. Reduce the heat to low. Cover and cook for 20 minutes or until the rice is tender.

3. Stir in the soup. Cook for 2 minutes or until the rice mixture is hot. Sprinkle with the cheese.

Makes 8 servings

Kitchen Tip: If you want a meatless side dish, substitute Swanson® Vegetable Broth (Regular **or** Certified Organic) for the Chicken Broth.

Harvest Salad

Prep: 10 minutes

2 packages (about 7 ounces **each**) mixed salad greens (about 8 cups)

2 cups cut-up fresh vegetables (red onions, cucumbers **and** carrots)

1 can (10¾ ounces) Campbell's® Condensed Tomato Soup (Regular **or** Healthy Request®)

¼ cup vegetable oil

¼ cup red wine vinegar

1 tablespoon honey **or** sugar

1 package (0.7 ounce) Italian salad dressing mix

2 cups your favorite Pepperidge Farm® croutons

¼ cup shelled pumpkin **or** sunflower seeds

1. Place the salad greens and vegetables into a large bowl.

2. Beat the soup, oil, vinegar, honey and salad dressing mix in a small bowl with a fork or whisk. Pour ¾ **cup** soup mixture over the salad mixture and toss to coat.

3. Arrange the salad on a serving platter. Top with the croutons and pumpkin seeds. Serve the salad with the remaining soup mixture.

Makes 8 servings

Mixed Greens and Fruit Salad with Warm Onion Vinaigrette

Prep: 10 minutes • **Cook:** 15 minutes

3 tablespoons olive oil
¼ cup finely chopped shallots **or** sweet onion
1 cup Swanson® Chicken Broth (Regular, Natural Goodness® or Certified Organic)
2 tablespoons balsamic vinegar
¼ cup packed brown sugar

1 tablespoon coarse-grain Dijon-style mustard
2 bags (5 to 8 ounces **each**) mixed salad greens
2 ripe pears **or** apples, thinly sliced (about 2 cups)
½ cup dried cherries **or** cranberries
¼ cup pecans, toasted
Crumbled blue cheese (optional)

1. Heat **1 tablespoon** oil in a 2-quart saucepan over medium heat. Add the shallots and cook for 3 minutes or until they're tender.

2. Stir the broth, vinegar, brown sugar and mustard in the saucepan and heat to a boil. Cook for 5 minutes or until the mixture is slightly reduced. Remove the saucepan from the heat. Beat the remaining oil into the broth mixture with a fork or whisk. Remove the saucepan from the heat and cool slightly.

3. Toss the salad greens with ½ **cup** dressing in a large bowl. Arrange the greens on a serving platter. Top with the pears, cherries, pecans and cheese, if desired. Serve with the remaining dressing.

Makes 8 servings

Spaghetti Squash Alfredo

Prep: 10 minutes • **Cook:** 55 minutes

1 medium spaghetti squash
   (about 3 pounds)
1 can (10¾ ounces) Campbell's®
   Condensed Cream of Celery
   Soup (Regular **or** 98% Fat Free)
¾ cup water

¼ cup milk
1 cup shredded lowfat Swiss
   cheese (about 4 ounces)
2 tablespoons grated Parmesan
   cheese
   Chopped fresh parsley **or** chives

1. Pierce the squash with a fork.

2. Bake at 350°F. for 50 minutes or until the squash is fork-tender. Cut the squash in half and scoop out and discard the seeds. Scrape the flesh with a fork to separate the spaghetti-like strands.

3. Heat the soup, water and milk in a 3-quart saucepan over medium heat to a boil. Stir in the Swiss cheese. Add the squash and toss to coat. Sprinkle with the Parmesan cheese and parsley.

Makes 5 servings

Broccoli & Noodles Supreme

Prep: 10 minutes • **Cook:** 25 minutes

3 cups **uncooked** medium egg
   noodles
2 cups fresh **or** frozen broccoli
   flowerets

1 can (10¾ ounces) Campbell's®
   Condensed Cream of Chicken
   Soup (Regular **or** 98% Fat Free)
½ cup sour cream
⅓ cup grated Parmesan cheese
⅛ teaspoon ground black pepper

1. Cook the noodles according to the package directions. Add the broccoli for the last 5 minutes of cooking time. Drain the noodle mixture well in a colander. Return the noodle mixture to the saucepan.

2. Stir the soup, sour cream, cheese and black pepper in the saucepan and cook over medium heat until the mixture is hot and bubbling, stirring often.

Makes 5 servings

Mozzarella Zucchini Skillet

Prep: 10 minutes • **Cook:** 15 minutes

2 tablespoons vegetable oil
5 medium zucchini, sliced
   (about 7½ cups)
1 medium onion, chopped
   (about ½ cup)
¼ teaspoon garlic powder **or**
   2 cloves garlic, minced

1½ cups Prego® Traditional Italian
   Sauce **or** Prego® Organic
   Tomato & Basil Italian Sauce
½ cup shredded mozzarella cheese
   or Cheddar cheese

1. Heat the oil in a 12-inch skillet over medium-high heat. Add the zucchini, onion and garlic powder and cook until the vegetables are tender-crisp.

2. Stir the Italian sauce into the skillet and heat through.

3. Sprinkle with the cheese. Cover and cook until the cheese melts.

Makes 7 servings

Corn and Black-Eyed Pea Salad

Prep: 15 minutes • **Chill:** 4 hours

1 bag (16 ounces) frozen whole
   kernel corn, thawed
   (about 3 cups)
1 can (about 15 ounces) black-eyed
   peas, rinsed and drained
1 large green pepper, chopped
   (about 1 cup)

1 medium onion, chopped
   (about ½ cup)
½ cup chopped fresh cilantro leaves
1 jar (16 ounces) Pace® Picante
   Sauce

1. Place the corn, peas, green pepper, onion and cilantro into a medium bowl. Add the picante sauce and stir to coat.

2. Cover and refrigerate for 4 hours. Stir before serving.

Makes 8 servings

Kitchen Tip: To make ahead, prepare salad as directed. Cover and refrigerate overnight. Stir before serving.

Oven-Roasted Root Vegetables

Prep: 35 minutes • **Cook:** 50 minutes

Vegetable cooking spray
3 medium red potatoes (about 1 pound), cut into 1-inch pieces
2 cups fresh **or** frozen whole baby carrots
1 pound celery root (celeriac), peeled and cut into 1-inch pieces (about 2 cups)
1 rutabaga (about 3 pounds), peeled and cut into 1-inch pieces (about 6 cups)

2 medium red onions, cut into 8 wedges **each**
2 medium parsnips, peeled and cut into 1-inch pieces (about 1½ cups)
5 cloves garlic, cut into thin slices
1 tablespoon chopped fresh rosemary leaves **or** fresh thyme leaves
1 tablespoon olive oil
1 cup Swanson® Vegetable Broth (Regular **or** Certified Organic)

1. Heat the oven to 425°F. Spray a 17×11-inch roasting pan or shallow baking sheet with the cooking spray.

2. Stir the potatoes, carrots, celery root, rutabaga, onions, parsnips, garlic, rosemary and oil in the prepared pan. Roast the vegetables for 30 minutes. Pour the broth over the vegetables and stir.

3. Roast for 20 minutes or until the vegetables are fork-tender.

Makes 8 servings

Cheddar Broccoli Bake

Prep: 10 minutes • **Bake:** 30 minutes

1 can (10¾ ounces) Campbell's®
    Condensed Cheddar Cheese
    Soup
½ cup milk

Dash ground black pepper
4 cups cooked broccoli flowerets
1⅓ cups French fried onions

1. Stir the soup, milk, black pepper, broccoli and ⅔ **cup** onions in a 1½-quart casserole.

2. Bake at 350°F. for 25 minutes or until the mixture is hot and bubbling. Stir.

3. Top with the remaining onions. Bake for 5 minutes or until the onions are golden.

Makes 6 servings

Roasted Potatoes with Thyme

Prep: 5 minutes • **Cook:** 35 minutes

4 medium potatoes (about 1¼ pounds), sliced ¼-inch thick	¼ teaspoon ground black pepper
1 teaspoon dried thyme leaves, crushed	3 tablespoons vegetable oil
	1 jar (12 ounces) Franco-American® Chicken Gravy

1. Heat the oven to 400°F. Stir the potatoes, thyme, black pepper and oil in a 17×11-inch roasting pan or shallow baking sheet.

2. Roast the potatoes for 20 minutes. Turn the potatoes. Roast for 15 minutes more or until the potatoes are fork-tender and browned.

3. Heat the gravy and serve with the potatoes.

Makes 4 servings

Sweet Treats

Apple Strudel

Thaw: 40 minutes · **Prep:** 30 minutes · **Bake:** 35 minutes · **Cool:** 20 minutes

- ½ **of a 17.3-ounce package Pepperidge Farm® Puff Pastry Sheets (1 sheet)**
- 1 **egg**
- 1 **tablespoon water**
- 2 **tablespoons granulated sugar**
- 1 **tablespoon all-purpose flour**
- ¼ **teaspoon ground cinnamon**
- 2 **large Granny Smith apples, peeled, cored and thinly sliced**
- 2 **tablespoons raisins**
  Confectioners' sugar (optional)

1. Thaw the pastry sheet at room temperature for 40 minutes or until it's easy to handle. Heat the oven to 375°F. Lightly grease a baking sheet. Beat the egg and water in a small bowl with a fork.

2. Stir the granulated sugar, flour and cinnamon in a medium bowl. Add the apples and raisins and toss to coat.

3. Unfold the pastry sheet on a lightly floured surface. Roll the pastry sheet into a 16×12-inch rectangle. With the short side facing you, spoon the apple mixture onto the bottom half of the pastry sheet to within 1 inch of the edges. Starting at the short side, roll up like a jelly roll. Tuck the ends under to seal. Place seam-side down on the baking sheet. Brush the pastry with the egg mixture. Cut several 2-inch-long slits 2 inches apart on the top.

4. Bake for 35 minutes or until the pastry is golden. Cool on the baking sheet on a wire rack for 20 minutes. Sprinkle with the confectioners' sugar, if desired.

Makes 6 servings

Kitchen Tip: Make sure to toss the apples and raisins in Step 2 until they're evenly coated with the flour mixture. The flour helps to thicken the juices released by the apples as they cook.

Sweet Potato Pie

Prep: 15 minutes • **Bake:** 1 hour • **Cool:** 3 hours

3 large sweet potatoes, peeled and
   cut into cubes (about 3 cups)
¼ cup heavy cream
1 can (10¾ ounces) Campbell's®
   Condensed Tomato Soup

1 cup packed brown sugar
3 eggs
1 teaspoon vanilla extract
½ teaspoon ground cinnamon
½ teaspoon ground nutmeg
1 (9-inch) frozen pie crust

1. Heat the oven to 350°F.

2. Place potatoes into a 3-quart saucepan and add water to cover. Heat over medium-high heat to a boil. Reduce the heat to low. Cover and cook for 10 minutes or until the potatoes are tender. Drain the potatoes well in a colander.

3. Place the potatoes and heavy cream into a large bowl. Beat with an electric mixer on medium speed until the mixture is fluffy. Beat in the soup, brown sugar, eggs, vanilla extract, cinnamon and nutmeg. Pour the potato mixture into the pie crust and place onto a baking sheet.

4. Bake for 1 hour or until set. Let the pie cool in the pan on a wire rack for 3 hours.

Makes 8 servings

Kitchen Tip: Substitute 1¾ **cups** drained and mashed canned sweet potatoes for the fresh mashed sweet potatoes.

Bread and Butter Pudding

Prep: 10 minutes • **Stand:** 5 minutes • **Bake:** 40 minutes

½ cup (1 stick) butter, softened
1 loaf (16 ounces) Pepperidge
   Farm® Toasting White Bread
2 teaspoons ground cinnamon
¼ cup currants
6 eggs

2 egg yolks
½ cup granulated sugar
4 cups heavy cream
2 cups milk
1 teaspoon vanilla extract
2 tablespoons packed brown sugar

1. Heat the oven to 350°F. Grease a 3-quart shallow baking dish with **2 tablespoons** butter.

2. Spread the remaining butter on the bread slices. Cut the bread slices in half diagonally. Arrange **half** the bread slices in the baking dish, overlapping as needed. Sprinkle with **half** of the cinnamon and **half** of the currants. Repeat with the remaining bread slices, cinnamon and currants.

3. Beat the eggs, egg yolks and granulated sugar with a fork or whisk. Heat the cream and milk in a 2-quart saucepan over low heat until the mixture is warm. Stir in the vanilla extract. Stir some of the cream mixture into the egg mixture. Stir the egg mixture in the saucepan.

4. Pour the egg mixture over the bread. Let stand for 5 minutes. Sprinkle with the brown sugar.

5. Bake for 40 minutes or until set.

Makes 8 servings

Kitchen Tip: To make ahead, prepare the recipe through step 2 up to 1 day ahead but do not bake. Cover and refrigerate overnight. Bake at 350°F. for 40 minutes or until the custard is set.

Chocolate and Coconut Cream Fondue

Prep: 5 minutes • **Cook:** 10 minutes

1 **can (15 ounces) cream of coconut**
1 **package (12 ounces) semi-sweet chocolate pieces (about 2 cups)**
2 **tablespoons rum or 1 teaspoon rum extract**

Assorted Dippers: Assorted Pepperidge Farm® Cookies, whole strawberries, banana chunks, dried pineapple pieces **and** fresh pineapple chunks

1. Heat the cream of coconut, chocolate and rum, if desired, in a 2-quart heavy saucepan over low heat until the mixture is melted and smooth, stirring occasionally.

2. Pour the chocolate mixture into a fondue pot or slow cooker. Serve warm with *Assorted Dippers*.

Makes 24 servings

Kitchen Tip: Any remaining fondue can be used as an ice cream or dessert topping. Cover and refrigerate in an airtight container. Heat in a 2-quart saucepan over medium heat until the mixture is warm.

I'm Dreamy for a White Chocolate Fondue

Prep: 5 minutes • **Cook:** 10 minutes

⅓ cup heavy cream
1 tablespoon orange-flavored liqueur **or** ½ teaspoon orange extract
1 package (about 12 ounces) white chocolate pieces

Assorted Dippers: Assorted Pepperidge Farm® Cookies, whole strawberries, banana chunks, dried pineapple pieces **and/or** fresh pineapple chunks

1. Heat the heavy cream, liqueur and chocolate in a 1-quart heavy saucepan over low heat until the mixture is melted and smooth, stirring occasionally.

2. Pour the mixture into a fondue pot or slow cooker. Serve warm with the *Assorted Dippers*.

Makes 12 servings

Super Chunky Fudge

Prep: 15 minutes • **Cook:** 10 minutes • **Chill:** 2 hours

1 bag (5.1 ounces) Pepperidge Farm® 100 Calorie Pack Chocolate Chunk Cookies, coarsely crumbled (about 2 cups)
1 cup miniature marshmallows

Vegetable cooking spray
3 cups (18 ounces) semi-sweet chocolate pieces
1 can (14 ounces) sweetened condensed milk
⅛ teaspoon salt
1 teaspoon vanilla extract

1. Reserve ½ **cup** crumbled cookies and ¼ **cup** marshmallows. Line an 8-inch square baking pan with foil. Spray the foil with cooking spray. Heat the chocolate, milk and salt in a 2-quart saucepan over low heat until the chocolate melts, stirring often.

2. Remove the chocolate mixture from the heat and stir in remaining crumbled cookies, remaining marshmallows and vanilla extract. Spread the mixture evenly into the prepared pan. Press the reserved cookies and marshmallows into top of fudge.

3. Refrigerate for 2 hours or until firm. Remove fudge from pan and peel away foil. Cut into 16 squares. Wrap in foil. Store in the refrigerator.

Makes 16 pieces

Kitchen Tip: To wrap for gift-giving, arrange each piece of fudge in a decorative paper cupcake liner. Wrap with colored plastic wrap and close with twist-tie or ribbon.

Chocolate Goldfish® Pretzel Clusters

Prep: 5 minutes • **Cook:** 1 minute • **Chill:** 30 minutes

1 package (12 ounces) semi-sweet chocolate pieces (about 2 cups)

2½ cups Pepperidge Farm® Pretzel Goldfish® Crackers

1 container (4 ounces) multi-colored nonpareils

1. Line a baking sheet with waxed paper. Place the chocolate into a microwavable bowl. Microwave on HIGH for 1 minute. Stir. Microwave at 15-second intervals, stirring after each, until the chocolate is melted and smooth. Add the Goldfish® crackers and stir to coat.

2. Drop the chocolate mixture by tablespoonfuls onto the baking sheet. Sprinkle the clusters with the nonpareils.

3. Refrigerate for 30 minutes or until the clusters are firm. Store in the refrigerator.

Makes 24 servings

Kitchen Tip: To wrap for gift-giving, arrange the clusters in a small candy box lined with colored plastic wrap.

Citrus Fruit Tarts

Prep: 20 minutes · **Bake:** 25 minutes

2 packages (10 ounces **each**) Pepperidge Farm® Puff Pastry Shells

1 package (8 ounces) cream cheese, softened

1 tablespoon sugar

2 tablespoons orange juice

2 teaspoons grated orange zest

1 cup thawed frozen whipped topping

6 strawberries, cut in half

3 peeled orange slices, cut into quarters

1 kiwi, peeled and cut into 12 chunks

½ cup apricot preserves, warmed

1. Heat the oven to 400°F. Bake, cool and remove the "tops" of the pastry shells according to the package directions.

2. Beat the cream cheese, sugar, orange juice and orange zest in a medium bowl with a fork or whisk until the mixture is smooth. Fold in the whipped topping.

3. Spoon **about 3 tablespoons** cream cheese mixture into **each** pastry shell. Divide the fruit among the filled pastry shells. Brush the fruit with the preserves. Serve immediately or cover and refrigerate for up to 4 hours.

Makes 12 servings

Kitchen Tip: To soften the cream cheese, remove the wrapper and place the cream cheese on a microwavable plate. Microwave on HIGH for 15 seconds or until it's softened.

Mini Chocolate Cookie Cheesecakes

Prep: 20 minutes · **Bake:** 20 minutes · **Cool:** 1 hour · **Chill:** 2 hours

16 foil baking cups (2½ inch)
2 packages (4.9 ounces **each**) Pepperidge Farm® Mini Milano® Cookies

2 packages (8 ounces **each**) cream cheese, softened
½ cup sugar
2 eggs
½ teaspoon vanilla extract

1. Heat the oven to 350°F. Place the foil baking cups into **16** (2½-inch) muffin-pan cups. Place **2** cookies in the bottom of **each** cup. Cut the remaining cookies in half crosswise.

2. Beat the cream cheese, sugar, eggs and vanilla extract in a medium bowl with an electric mixer on medium speed until the mixture is smooth. Spoon the cheese mixture into the baking cups. Insert **2** cookie halves, with the cut-side down, into the cheese mixture of **each** cup.

3. Bake for 20 minutes or until the filling is set. Cool on a wire rack for 1 hour. Refrigerate the cheesecakes for 2 hours or until chilled.

Makes 16 servings

Kitchen Tip: You can also make this recipe with Pepperidge Farm® Mini Mint Milano® Cookies instead of the original variety.

Chocolate Cherry Ice Cream Cake

Prep: 10 minutes • **Freeze:** 2 hours 15 minutes

1 package (6 ounces) Pepperidge Farm® Milano® Distinctive Cookies
1 container (1.75 quarts) black cherry ice cream
2 jars (17 ounces **each**) chocolate ice cream sauce

1 container (1.75 quarts) vanilla ice cream
Sweetened whipped cream for garnish
Frozen pitted dark cherries, thawed for garnish

1. Stand **10** of the cookies on their sides along the edge of a 9-inch springform pan, forming a ring. Coarsely chop the remaining cookies.

2. Spoon the black cherry ice cream into the pan and spread into an even layer. Spoon **1** jar of the chocolate sauce over the ice cream. Sprinkle with the coarsely chopped cookies. Freeze for 15 minutes.

3. Evenly spread the vanilla ice cream over the cookie layer. Pour the remaining chocolate sauce in the center, spreading into a circle to within 1 inch of the edge. Pipe the whipped cream around the top edge. Freeze for 2 hours more or until firm.

4. Place cherries on top of the cake just before serving.

Makes 10 servings

Kitchen Tip: Ice cream is easier to spread when it's slightly softened. Let the ice cream sit at room temperature for about 10 minutes and spread gently with a flexible spatula to make an even layer.

Southern Pecan Crisps

Thaw: 40 minutes • **Prep:** 25 minutes • **Bake:** 12 minutes

½ of a 17.3-ounce package Pepperidge Farm® Frozen Puff Pastry Sheets (1 sheet)

½ cup packed brown sugar
⅓ cup chopped pecans
2 tablespoons butter, melted
Confectioners' sugar

1. Thaw the pastry sheet at room temperature for 40 minutes or until it's easy to handle. Heat the oven to 400°F. Mix the brown sugar and the pecans with the butter in a small bowl.

2. Unfold the pastry sheet on a lightly floured surface. Roll the sheet into a 15×12-inch rectangle. Cut the pastry into **20** (3-inch) squares. Press the squares into bottoms of 3-inch muffin-pan cups. Place **1 heaping teaspoon** pecan mixture in center of **each** cup.

3. Bake for 12 minutes or until golden. Remove from the pans and cool on a wire rack. Sprinkle the pastries with confectioners' sugar before serving.

Makes 20 pastries

Kitchen Tip: Wrap unused pastry sheets in plastic wrap or foil and return to the freezer. Thawed pastry sheets will be cool to the touch and will unfold without breaking. Thawed pastry sheets can be refrigerated up to 2 days.

Quick & Easy Berry Shortcakes

Prep: 10 minutes · **Bake:** 40 minutes   **Cool:** 1 hour 30 minutes

1 box (16 ounces) angel food cake mix

1¼ cups Diet V8 Splash® Berry Blend Juice

6 cups cut-up fresh strawberries, blueberries **and** raspberries

1½ cups thawed light whipped topping

1. Heat the oven to 350°F. Prepare the cake mix according to the package directions, substituting juice for the water. Pour the batter into a 10-inch tube pan.

2. Bake for 40 minutes or until the crust is golden brown and cracked. Hang pan upside down on a heatproof glass bottle for about 1½ hours to cool completely.

3. Cut the cake into **24** slices. For each serving, place **1** cake slice on a serving plate, top with ¼ **cup** berries and **1 tablespoon** whipped topping, top with another cake slice, ¼ **cup** berries and **1 tablespoon** whipped topping. Repeat with remaining cake slices, berries and whipped topping.

Makes 12 servings

Mandarin Orange Ginger Cream Puffs

Prep: 20 minutes • **Bake:** 15 minutes   **Cool:** 30 minutes

1 package (10 ounces) Pepperidge Farm® Frozen Puff Pastry Shells
1 package (about 3½ ounces) vanilla instant pudding & pie filling mix
1 cup milk
½ teaspoon ground ginger
1½ cups sweetened whipped cream
1 can (11 ounces) Mandarin orange segments, drained

2 tablespoons apple jelly, melted
Confectioners' sugar
Orange peel
Assorted fresh berries (raspberries, blackberries **and/or** blueberries)
Fresh herb leaves (thyme, lavender, rosemary **or** mint)

1. Heat the oven to 400°F. Bake and cool the pastry shells according to the package directions.

2. Prepare the pudding mix according to the package directions **except** use **1 cup** milk and add the ginger. Fold in the whipped cream.

3. Split the pastries into **2** layers. Place **4** orange segments on each bottom layer. Using a pastry bag fitted with a large fluted decorating tip, pipe ½ **cup** pudding mixture on each. Top with top layers and **3** orange segments. Serve immediately, or cover and refrigerate up to 4 hours. Just before serving, brush the jelly over the orange segments. Sift the sugar over the pastries. Top with orange peel. Garnish with berries and herbs as desired.

Makes 6 servings

Kitchen Tip: For 1½ **cups** sweetened whipped cream, beat ¾ **cup** heavy cream, **2 tablespoons** sugar and ¼ **teaspoon** vanilla extract in a chilled medium bowl using an electric mixer at high speed until stiff peaks form.

Beverages

Frosted Citrus Green Tea

Prep: 15 minutes • **Chill/Freeze:** 1 hour 30 minutes

4 **cups Diet V8 Splash® Tropical Blend Juice Drink, chilled**
4 **cups strong brewed green tea**
   Fresh mint sprigs (optional)
   Lemon slices (optional)

1. Pour **2 cups** of the juice drink into **1** ice cube tray. Freeze for 1 hour 30 minutes or until it's frozen.

2. Stir the remaining juice drink and tea in a pitcher and refrigerate for at least 1 hour 30 minutes.

3. Unmold the cubes and place **3 to 4** cubes in each of **6** glasses. Pour the tea mixture into **each** glass. Serve with mint and lemon, if desired.

Makes 6 servings

Orange Mist

Prep: 5 minutes

6 cups V8® 100% Vegetable Juice
1 can (6 ounces) frozen orange
   juice concentrate, thawed

1½ cups seltzer water **or** orange-
   flavored seltzer water
   Ice cubes

Stir the vegetable juice and orange juice concentrate in a large pitcher. Add the seltzer water. Serve over ice.

Makes 10 servings

Jump Start Smoothie

Prep: 5 minutes

2 cups V8 Splash® Mango Peach
   Juice Drink, chilled
1 cup low-fat vanilla yogurt

2 cups frozen whole strawberries
   or raspberries

Put all the ingredients in a blender. Cover and blend until they're smooth. Serve immediately.

Makes 4 servings

Lemon Sangrita Punch

Prep: 10 minutes

2 cups V8® 100% Vegetable Juice, chilled
1 container (64 ounces) refrigerated lemonade
1 tablespoon Worcestershire sauce

2 lemons, thinly sliced
2 limes, thinly sliced
1 orange, thinly sliced
Ice cubes

1. Stir the vegetable juice, lemonade and Worcestershire, if desired, and the lemon, lime and orange slices in an 8-quart punch bowl.

2. Serve immediately or refrigerate until serving time.

3. Pour into ice-filled tall glasses.

Makes 20 servings

Kitchen Tip: For added "kick" to the punch, add **2 cups** vodka.

Bellini Splash

Prep: 5 minutes

½ **cup V8 Splash® Mango Peach**
    Juice Drink, chilled
¼ **cup peach nectar, chilled**

1 **cup champagne, sparkling wine**
    or sparkling cider, chilled

1. Stir the juice drink and nectar in a **1 cup** measure.

2. Divide the mixture between **2** fluted champagne glasses. Pour in the champagne.

3. Serve immediately.

Makes 2 servings

Tropical Freeze

Prep: 10 minutes

1 **bottle (16 ounces) V8 Splash®
Tropical Blend Juice Drink,
chilled**

1 **pint orange or mango sherbet or
vanilla ice cream**
1 **cup crushed ice**
2 **medium bananas, sliced**

1. Put the juice drink, sherbet, ice and ½ of the bananas in a blender.

2. Cover and blend until the mixture is smooth. Garnish with the remaining banana slices. Serve immediately.

Makes 4 servings

Spicy Mary Martini

Prep: 5 minutes

2 cans (5.5 ounces **each**) Spicy Hot
   V8® Vegetable Juice
6 tablespoons pepper-flavored
   vodka

Dash chipotle hot pepper sauce
   or to taste
2 cups ice cubes
   Seasoned salt
2 stalks celery

1. Put the vegetable juice, vodka, pepper sauce and ice in a cocktail shaker.
Cover and shake until blended.

2. Strain into **2** chilled tall glasses rimmed with seasoned salt, if desired.

3. Serve with the celery.

Makes 2 servings

Salsa Sipper

Prep: 5 minutes

**1 can (5.5 ounces) V8® 100%
    Vegetable Juice or Spicy Hot
    V8® Vegetable Juice
1½ ounces vodka**

**1 teaspoon lemon juice
    Dash Worcestershire sauce
    Dash hot pepper sauce
    Celery stalk for garnish**

Stir the vegetable juice, vodka, lemon juice, Worcestershire and hot pepper sauce in a small pitcher. Serve over ice. Garnish with a celery stalk.

Makes 1 serving

Russian Witches' Brew

Prep: 5 minutes • **Cook:** 15 minutes

2 bottles (16 fluid ounces **each**)
   V8 Splash® Tropical Blend Juice
   Drink (4 cups)

4 cups strong brewed tea*
11 cinnamon sticks
8 whole cloves

1. Stir the juice drink, tea, **3** cinnamon sticks and cloves in a 4-quart saucepot. Heat over medium-high heat to a boil. Reduce the heat to medium-low and cook for 10 minutes. Remove the cinnamon sticks and cloves.

2. Place remaining cinnamon sticks in **8** mugs and fill with juice mixture.

3. Serve immediately or keep it warm in the saucepot over very low heat.

Makes 8 servings

*Strong brewed tea:** Heat **4 cups** of water in a 2-quart saucepan over high heat to a boil. Remove the pan from the heat. Add **8** tea bags and let them steep for 5 minutes. Remove the tea bags.

Kitchen Tip: Recipe may be doubled or tripled.

Berry Rum Toddies

Prep: 5 minutes • **Cook:** 5 minutes

1 bottle (16 ounces) V8 Splash®
   Berry Blend Juice Drink (2 cups)
¼ cup dark spiced **or** regular rum

½ teaspoon ground cinnamon
¼ teaspoon ground ginger
2 cinnamon sticks

1. Heat the juice drink, rum, cinnamon and ginger in a 1-quart saucepan to a boil over medium heat and cook for 5 minutes, stirring occasionally.

2. Pour the juice mixture into **2** mugs.

3. Serve immediately with the cinnamon sticks.

Makes 2 servings

Tropical Champagne Ice

Prep: 15 minutes • **Freeze:** 3 hours

6 cups V8 Splash® Tropical Blend Juice Drink, chilled	**1 teaspoon grated orange peel (optional)**
1 bottle (750 mL) champagne or other sparkling wine, chilled	**4½ cups cut-up fresh fruit (mango, papaya or pineapple)**

1. Stir the juice drink, champagne and orange peel, if desired, in a 13×9×2-inch metal baking pan.

2. Cover the pan and freeze it for 3 hours, stirring with a fork every hour.

3. Scoop about ½ **cup** of the champagne ice into a stemmed glass or dessert glass. Top with the fruit. Serve immediately.

Makes 18 servings

Kitchen Tip: If you have any leftover ice, wrap the pan with plastic wrap and store it in the freezer. When you want to serve it, remove it from the freezer about 5 minutes before serving to allow it to soften a bit before scooping.

Index

Appetizers

Bloody Fingers 94

Caponata Appetizers 19

Cheesy Vegetable Triangles....... 14

Fiesta Tortilla Roll-Ups 20

Game-Winning Drumsticks...... 21

Goblin's Toes 96

Grilled Bruschetta 13

Hot Artichoke Dip.................... 12

Italiano Fondue 6

Layered Pizza Dip...................... 4

October Dinner Fondue 97

Pizza Fondue 95

Porcupine Meatballs 9

Salmon Bites 15

Sausage-Stuffed Mushrooms..... 17

Seafood & Cilantro
    Sandwiches........................16

Shrimp Dip 8

Single-Serve Southwest
    Dip Cups 18

Spicy Grilled Quesadillas......... 11

Tex-Mex Toasts......................... 10

Walnut-Cheddar Ball 7

Warm French Onion Dip
    with Crusty Bread............... 22

Warm Spinach Dip 23

Apple Strudel.............................. 112

Autumn Pork Chops...................... 50

Baked Chicken & Cheese Risotto... 68

Balsamic Glazed Salmon............... 56

Barbecued Pork Spareribs............. 69

Beef

Beef & Bean Burritos................ 45

Beef Stroganoff......................... 60

French Onion Burgers 48

Pan-Seared Beef Steaks with
    Garlic Red Wine Gravy....... 75

Sirloin Steak Olé 71

Slow-Cooked Autumn Brisket... 62

Tangy Grilled Beef 58

Beef & Bean Burritos 45

Beef Stroganoff 60

Bellini Splash............................... 131

Berry Rum Toddies....................... 136

Beverages

Bellini Splash 131

Berry Rum Toddies 136

Frosted Citrus Green Tea 126

Jump Start Smoothie............... 129

Lemon Sangrita Punch 130

Orange Mist........................... 128

Russian Witches' Brew 135

Salsa Sipper 134

Spicy Mary Martini 133

Tropical Champagne Ice 137

Tropical Freeze 132

Bloody Fingers 94

Bread and Butter Pudding 115

Broccoli & Noodles Supreme 106

Broccoli and Pasta Bianco 67

Caponata Appetizers 19

Cheddar Broccoli Bake 110

Cheesy Chicken & Rice
    Casserole 76

Cheesy Mexican Bread 83

Cheesy Vegetable Triangles 14

Chicken & Black Bean
    Quesadillas 43

Chicken & Stuffing Skillet 63

Chicken Broccoli Divan 73

Chicken Nacho Tacos 77

Chicken Scampi 59

Chilis & Chowders

Chipotle Chili 36

Shrimp & Corn Chowder
    with Sun-Dried Tomatoes 37

Simply Special Seafood
    Chowder 30

Slow Cooker Tuscan Beef Stew ...34

Chipotle Chili 36

Chocolate and Coconut
    Cream Fondue 116

Chocolate Cherry Ice
    Cream Cake 122

Chocolate Goldfish®
    Pretzel Clusters 119

Citrus Fruit Tarts 120

Corn and Black-Eyed Pea Salad ... 108

Crab and Asparagus Risotto 98

Cranberry Dijon Pork Chops 65

Creamy 3-Cheese Pasta 74

Creamy Beet Soup 28

Creamy Citrus Tomato
    Soup with Pesto Croutons 31

Creamy Irish Potato Soup 35

Desserts

Apple Strudel 112

Bread and Butter Pudding 115

Chocolate and Coconut
    Cream Fondue 116

Chocolate Cherry Ice
    Cream Cake 122

Chocolate Goldfish® Pretzel
    Clusters 119

Citrus Fruit Tarts 120

I'm Dreamy for a White
    Chocolate Fondue 117

Mandarin Orange Ginger
    Cream Puffs 125

Mini Chocolate Cookie
Cheesecakes...................... 121

Quick & Easy Berry
Shortcakes 124

Southern Pecan Crisps............ 123

Super Chunky Fudge.............. 118

Sweet Potato Pie 114

Eggplant Tomato Gratin 85

Fiesta Tortilla Roll-Ups................... 20

Fish & Shellfish

Balsamic Glazed Salmon 56

Fish & Vegetable Skillet............ 70

Grilled Fish Steaks with
Chunky Tomato Sauce 44

Italian Fish Fillets 42

New Orleans Shrimp Toss 52

Poached Halibut
with Pineapple Salsa........... 55

Fish & Vegetable Skillet................. 70

French Onion Burgers.................... 48

Frosted Citrus Green Tea 126

Game-Winning Drumsticks 21

German Potato Salad..................... 78

Glazed Snow Peas and Carrots..... 100

Goblin's Toes................................ 96

Green Bean Casserole 80

Grilled Bruschetta.......................... 13

Grilled Fish Steaks
with Chunky Tomato Sauce 44

Grilled Pork in Pita 46

Harvest Salad 103

Hearty Bean & Barley Soup 38

Heavenly Sweet Potatoes.............. 87

Herb Roasted Turkey..................... 86

Holiday Potato Pancakes............... 84

Hot Artichoke Dip 12

I'm Dreamy for a White
Chocolate Fondue................. 117

Italian Chicken Pasta Salad 64

Italian Fish Fillets........................... 42

Italiano Fondue.............................. 6

Jump Start Smoothie 129

Lamb

Moroccan Lamb Stew 66

Layered Chicken Parmesan 49

Layered Cranberry Walnut
Stuffing 89

Layered Pizza Dip 4

Lemon Herb Broccoli Casserole......90

Lemon Sangrita Punch................. 130

Loaded Baked Potato Casserole 92

Longevity Noodle Soup 82

Mandarin Orange Ginger
    Cream Puffs 125

Mediterranean Chop Salad 101

Mini Chocolate Cookie
    Cheesecakes 121

Mixed Greens and Fruit
    Salad with Warm Onion
    Vinaigrette 104

Monterey Chicken Fajitas 57

Moroccan Lamb Stew 66

Mozzarella Zucchini Skillet 107

New Orleans Shrimp Toss 52

October Dinner Fondue 97

Orange Mist 128

Oven-Roasted Root Vegetables 109

Pan-Seared Beef Steaks with
    Garlic Red Wine Gravy 75

Pasta

Broccoli and Pasta Bianco 67

Creamy 3-Cheese Pasta 74

Pizza Fondue 95

Poached Halibut with
    Pineapple Salsa 55

Porcupine Meatballs 9

Pork

Autumn Pork Chops 50

Barbecued Pork Spareribs 69

Cranberry Dijon Pork Chops 65

Grilled Pork in Pita 46

Sausage-Stuffed Green
    Peppers 72

Poultry

Baked Chicken & Cheese
    Risotto 68

Cheesy Chicken & Rice
    Casserole 76

Chicken & Black Bean
    Quesadillas 43

Chicken & Stuffing Skillet 63

Chicken Broccoli Divan 73

Chicken Nacho Tacos 77

Chicken Scampi 59

Herb Roasted Turkey 86

Layered Chicken Parmesan 49

Monterey Chicken Fajitas 57

Rosemary Chicken &
    Mushroom Pasta 54

Saucy Cranberry Orange
    Chicken 51

Skillet Cheesy Chicken
    and Rice 53

Southwest Chicken with
    Fresh Greens 40

Tomato-Basil Chicken 47

Pumpkin Apple Mash 88

Quick & Easy Berry Shortcakes 124

Roasted Asparagus with
Lemon & Goat Cheese 81

Roasted Potatoes with Thyme 111

Roasted Tomato & Barley Soup 29

Rosemary Chicken &
Mushroom Pasta 54

Russian Witches' Brew 135

Salads

Corn and Black-Eyed
Pea Salad 108

Harvest Salad 103

Italian Chicken Pasta Salad 64

Mediterranean Chop Salad 101

Mixed Greens and Fruit
Salad with Warm
Onion Vinaigrette 104

Salmon Bites 15

Salsa Sipper 134

Saucy Cranberry Orange Chicken ...51

Sausage and Spinach Soup 27

Sausage-Stuffed Green Peppers 72

Sausage-Stuffed Mushrooms 17

Scalloped Apple Bake 93

Seafood & Cilantro Sandwiches 16

Shrimp & Corn Chowder
with Sun-Dried Tomatoes 37

Shrimp Dip 8

Side Dishes

Broccoli & Noodles
Supreme 106

Cheddar Broccoli Bake 110

Cheesy Mexican Bread 83

Crab and Asparagus Risotto 98

Eggplant Tomato Gratin 85

German Potato Salad 78

Glazed Snow Peas and
Carrots 100

Green Bean Casserole 80

Heavenly Sweet Potatoes 87

Holiday Potato Pancakes 84

Layered Cranberry Walnut
Stuffing 89

Lemon Herb Broccoli
Casserole 90

Loaded Baked Potato
Casserole 92

Mozzarella Zucchini Skillet 107

Oven-Roasted Root
Vegetables 109

Pumpkin Apple Mash 88

Roasted Asparagus with
Lemon & Goat Cheese 81

Roasted Potatoes with Thyme ... 111

Scalloped Apple Bake 93

Spaghetti Squash Alfredo 105

Swiss Vegetable Casserole 91

Toasted Corn & Sage
Harvest Risotto 102

Simply Special Seafood Chowder....30

Single-Serve Southwest Dip Cups....18

Sirloin Steak Olé............................ 71

Skillet Cheesy Chicken and Rice.... 53

Slow Cooker Tuscan Beef Stew 34

Slow-Cooked Autumn Brisket 62

Slow-Simmered Chicken
Rice Soup 32

Soups

Creamy Beet Soup.................... 28

Creamy Citrus Tomato Soup
with Pesto Croutons............ 31

Creamy Irish Potato Soup 35

Hearty Bean & Barley Soup...... 38

Longevity Noodle Soup............ 82

Roasted Tomato & Barley
Soup.................................. 29

Sausage and Spinach Soup....... 27

Slow-Simmered Chicken
Rice Soup.......................... 32

Southwestern Chicken &
White Bean Soup................ 24

Spaghetti Soup 39

Spicy Peanut Soup.................... 26

White Bean with Fennel Soup....33

Southern Pecan Crisps 123

Southwest Chicken
with Fresh Greens 40

Southwestern Chicken & White
Bean Soup 24

Spaghetti Soup.............................. 39

Spaghetti Squash Alfredo 105

Spicy Grilled Quesadillas 11

Spicy Mary Martini 133

Spicy Peanut Soup 26

Super Chunky Fudge 118

Sweet Potato Pie.......................... 114

Swiss Vegetable Casserole 91

Tangy Grilled Beef........................ 58

Tex-Mex Toasts 10

Toasted Corn & Sage Harvest
Risotto 102

Tomato-Basil Chicken.................... 47

Tropical Champagne Ice.............. 137

Tropical Freeze 132

Walnut-Cheddar Ball...................... 7

Warm French Onion Dip
with Crusty Bread 22

Warm Spinach Dip........................ 23

White Bean with Fennel Soup........ 33

Metric Conversion Chart

VOLUME MEASUREMENTS (dry)

⅛ teaspoon = 0.5 mL
¼ teaspoon = 1 mL
½ teaspoon = 2 mL
¾ teaspoon = 4 mL
1 teaspoon = 5 mL
1 tablespoon = 15 mL
2 tablespoons = 30 mL
¼ cup = 60 mL
⅓ cup = 75 mL
½ cup = 125 mL
⅔ cup = 150 mL
¾ cup = 175 mL
1 cup = 250 mL
2 cups = 1 pint = 500 mL
3 cups = 750 mL
4 cups = 1 quart = 1 L

VOLUME MEASUREMENTS (fluid)

1 fluid ounce (2 tablespoons) = 30 mL
4 fluid ounces (½ cup) = 125 mL
8 fluid ounces (1 cup) = 250 mL
12 fluid ounces (1½ cups) = 375 mL
16 fluid ounces (2 cups) = 500 mL

WEIGHTS (mass)

½ ounce = 15 g
1 ounce = 30 g
3 ounces = 90 g
4 ounces = 120 g
8 ounces = 225 g
10 ounces = 285 g
12 ounces = 360 g
16 ounces = 1 pound = 450 g

DIMENSIONS

1/16 inch = 2 mm
⅛ inch = 3 mm
¼ inch = 6 mm
½ inch = 1.5 cm
¾ inch = 2 cm
1 inch = 2.5 cm

OVEN TEMPERATURES

250°F = 120°C
275°F = 140°C
300°F = 150°C
325°F = 160°C
350°F = 180°C
375°F = 190°C
400°F = 200°C
425°F = 220°C
450°F = 230°C

BAKING PAN SIZES

Utensil	Size in Inches/Quarts	Metric Volume	Size in Centimeters
Baking or Cake Pan (square or rectangular)	8×8×2	2 L	20×20×5
	9×9×2	2.5 L	23×23×5
	12×8×2	3 L	30×20×5
	13×9×2	3.5 L	33×23×5
Loaf Pan	8×4×3	1.5 L	20×10×7
	9×5×3	2 L	23×13×7
Round Layer Cake Pan	8×1½	1.2 L	20×4
	9×1½	1.5 L	23×4
Pie Plate	8×1¼	750 mL	20×3
	9×1¼	1 L	23×3
Baking Dish or Casserole	1 quart	1 L	—
	1½ quarts	1.5 L	—
	2 quarts	2 L	—